OPPORTUNITIES FOR FAITH

OPPORTUNITIES FOR FAITH
Elements of a Modern Spirituality

KARL RAHNER

Translated by Edward Quinn

A Crossroad Book
THE SEABURY PRESS • NEW YORK

The Seabury Press
815 Second Avenue
New York, N.Y. 10017

Originally published as *Chancen des Glaubens*
Copyright © 1970 by Verlag Herder KG,
Freiburg-im-Breisgau

English translation copyright © 1974 by S.P.C.K.

Printed in the United States of America

LIBRARY OF CONGRESS CATALOGING IN
PUBLICATION DATA
Rahner, Karl, 1904-
    Opportunities for faith.

    Translation of Chancen des Glaubens.
    "A Crossroad book."
    Bibliography: p.
    1. Theology—Addresses, essays, lectures.   I. Title.
BR85.R22913   230   74-13973
ISBN 0-8164-1180-8

CONTENTS

ACKNOWLEDGEMENTS

Quotations from the *Revised Standard Version* of the Bible, copyrighted 1952 by the Division of Christian Education of the Natonal Council of Churches of Christ in the United States of America, are used by permission.

ABBREVIATIONS

Abbott = Documents of Vatican II; ed. Walter M. Abbott, s.j.; E.T.,
Joseph Gallagher. London, Geoffrey Chapman, and New
York, America Press, 1966.

DS   = *Enchiridion Symbolorum Definitionum et Declarationum de
Rebus Fidei et Morum.* First edited by H. Denzinger; revised
and augmented by Adolf Schonmetzer, s.j., Herder, Barce-
lona-Freiburg-Rome-New York, 1963.

AUTHOR'S PREFACE

We talk a lot today about the future of religion, the future of faith, of the Church; but this may well be merely a cloak to conceal our lack of courage. We want to project the future, although we gain it only by walking into it, full of hope. Although it is understandable that people should shrink in fear from such ultimate decisions, talking round and round the point can never be a substitute for understanding; and understanding is acquired only by believing, loving, committing ourselves, taking risks – in other words, precisely by winning it.

If we speak here of 'opportunities for faith' and not of 'the' opportunity for faith – which really amounts to the one opportunity of salvation for all – we mean that faith must be proved and tested and that it has many opportunities for this testing: mostly many small ones before a great one (the small ones being presumably the great ones and vice versa), mostly many thankless and exhausting opportunities before the one that really brings fulfilment and immediate satisfaction. But, since faith is tested by being placed at the service of one's neighbours, a Christian cannot expect any other opportunities. The Christian's selfless service to his neighbour, to freedom and peace, in overcoming hunger and violence, fulfils – so to speak, incidentally – our Lord's encouraging words about the light that is not put under a bushel, but that is put on the stand: 'Let your light so shine before men, that they may see your good works and give glory to your father who is in heaven' (Matt. 5.16). The deed of love liberates us to praise God.

Indications of such opportunities for faith, stimuli for practising a faith that takes risks and is ready to serve, tests of its credibility in the new community of salvation: this – no more and no less – is what these essays, however slight and limited, have to offer. They have emerged from conversations with modern men, in the course of preaching, and have grown out of reflection (which is the theologians' business) on how the 'ever valid' word of God is to be conveyed to this modern, sceptical, sensitive, secularized man. The sub-title, 'Elements of a modern spirituality', may appear to some to be too high-flown; but it is justified if this book succeeds in leading the reader to spiritual life, to the discernment of spirits, to the venture of a Christian life.

Münster 1 November 1970   KARL RAHNER

1
The Gospel Claim

RIGHTEOUSNESS
IN THE NEW TESTAMENT

For I tell you, unless your righteousness exceeds that of the scribes and Pharisees, you will never enter the kingdom of heaven. You have heard that it was said to the men of old, 'You shall not kill; and whoever kills shall be liable to judgment.' But I say to you that everyone who is angry with his brother shall be liable to judgment; whoever insults his brother shall be liable to the council, and whoever says, 'You fool!' shall be liable to the hell of fire. So if you are offering your gift at the altar, and there remember that your brother has something against you, leave your gift there before the altar and go; first to be reconciled to your brother, and then come and offer your gift (Matt. 5.20–4).

As you know, this passage of the Gospel is taken from the Sermon on the Mount and from the section bringing out the difference between the Old Law and the law of Jesus. I do not want so much to consider in detail this difference – on which Jesus had to insist – as to reflect on the internal attitude which is needed in order to get away from the morality of the Old Testament and enter into that of the New. We have to admit that what is typical of the Old Testament is still alive in us, inarticulately but truly: we understand and make our own the 'righteousness of the scribes and Pharisees' more easily than that which alone brings us into the kingdom of God, that which enables us to understand who God is and who enters into communion with him.

In my opinion it is impossible to understand the Sermon on the Mount at all unless we have the courage radically to call ourselves in question, precisely ourselves and not the others, ourselves and not merely some aspect of ourselves. We are always ready to defend ourselves even to our dying day (it is to be hoped that we don't continue to do so at that point). We want to have *our* righteousness, as Paul did before he became a Christian and learned to live as one. Throughout our lives, without using the actual words, we are saying in effect: 'God, I thank thee that I am not like other men', as Jesus makes the pharisee say in the temple (Luke 18.11). We are critical of many of our habits and ways but not of ourselves. And our critical reserve in regard to others is only a way of uncritically asserting ourselves in every dimension of our existence.

Have we ever seriously allowed for the possibility that we might not only have been mistaken in some of our opinions but that untruth might be rooted in the very depths of our existence? Can we really be so profoundly untruthful? given up to the untruth of lovelessness, of arrogance, of obstinacy? Is our truth that which involves us in incomprehensible, ineffable mystery? We admit of course that our moral life is imperfect and that we have our faults – as people say – and are even in love with them. But have we ever realized how our whole existence is imperilled, so that we no longer venture to make excuses, so that we are induced to silence, knowing only that we have to be forgiven and cannot forgive ourselves? Have we ever been seized with terror as we observed that we owed ourselves and not some particular object to another person, and that we remain in his debt without ever being able to repay him.

Have we ever asked ourselves whether the 'love' which we think we possess might perhaps be no more than a shrewd and calculated form of egoism? In a word: have we ever radically called in question our own internal set-up, down to the last detail? O God, we regard ourselves as reasonable, more or less clever and balanced people, as upright, industrious, helpful, as fine fellows, and we think that no one could have anything seriously against us. All this may well be true. But it is not yet really the attitude which we must adopt and constantly renew (we cannot talk of 'possessing' it) if we are to understand at all the impossible demands of the Sermon on the Mount: the radical calling in question of what we are, of that without which we think we could not exist at all; that capitulation which alone makes us free – free, that is, from ourselves.

If this is the sort of attitude necessary to understand the Sermon on the Mount, then no amount of talking about it is any guarantee of its existence. Indeed, talking may even be dangerous and at best merely shows that we have not overlooked the fact that there is a time and an hour in life when this type of attitude becomes a decisive factor in our salvation.

The fact that this attitude is required does not mean that it can be produced on any occasion or merely by thinking about it and willing it. The opposite attitudes – self-awareness, self-identification, self-confidence, reliance on oneself and one's resources – are so natural and appropriate in themselves that they seem to make what we are now talking about almost absurd and unrealizable. And if the attitude of which we are speaking were simply to extrude these other attitudes, which enable a person to accept life spontaneously, full of strength and self-confidence, then that person would become mentally disturbed and neurotic. He would not measure up to the demands of the Sermon on the Mount: he would not be a man who has really come to grips with himself. For in his capitulation this person is not less but mysteriously more than the one who unquestioningly assumes that he may and can be identical with himself. More, because all such harmony with oneself is underpinned (not simply abolished) by the abandonment of a final self-defence, of the self-defence of one's own truth before the silent mystery, of one's own goodness and security before an absolute demand which overtaxes us, judges us, and makes it impossible for us to want to be particularly good even in our own eyes.

It is only in a capitulation of this kind that we perceive what is really meant when we say 'God': we mean just that, he who is made known to us in this attitude, the real mystery, the absolute demand in person, the abyss into which man leaps without having plumbed its depths, as a Christian of course with faith, hope and love, so that by abandoning ourselves we are accepted, taken up and loved by this ineffable mystery. In this capitulation we accomplish what Jesus was destined to accomplish in his death.

When we read in the Gospel that our righteousness must not be that of the Pharisees, but, as Paul put it, the righteousness of God, we must not imagine that the Pharisees were hypocrites. We might well translate the sentence: If your righteousness is no better than that of *men*, than *our* righteousness that we have from ourselves, then you will not enter into God's kingdom. The Christian begins where truth becomes the mystery he worships, the core of life forgiveness by grace, the future God, the community God's Spirit, wisdom the folly of the cross, where the figure that remains constant in all our accounts becomes the God who cannot be manipulated; he begins where all this happens, without verbiage, in the simple routine of ordinary life in which we do what has to be done even if it seems to be fruitless.

Today for the first time we have with us the 'new' priests, those who have resolved to serve men and God in his Church. It is possible to become a Christian without being a priest. But this does not mean that the priesthood, for those who are called to it, is merely something added to their existence and growth as Christians. For those with a vocation it is in fact all one: they become Christians by becoming priests, and vice versa. By becoming a priest one enters on the terrible and blessed adventure of becoming a Christian. If this is what we want, then for a whole lifetime we are on the look-out for that moment, that chance, that call full of blessed-cruel challenge which suddenly comes upon us – we never know how and when – to get away from ourselves in freedom, because God wants to become our truth and our righteousness, our life and our future. It is of course clear that this moment (we never know if it is still to come or has already occurred) is a dying with Jesus Christ. And therefore at the present time too we proclaim the death of the Lord so that he may gain power over our life. But if what we are doing here in a sacred celebration should take hold on us in life, then we are Christians and priests. This is what we hope to become by the grace of God, we and the 'new' priests.

RADICAL FAITH IN ORDINARY LIFE

Jesus went away from there and came to his own country; and his disciples followed him. And on the sabbath he began to teach in the synagogue; and many who heard him were astonished, saying, 'Where did this man get all this? What is the wisdom given to him? What mighty works are wrought by his hands! Is not this the carpenter, the son of Mary and brother of James and Joses and Judas and Simon, and are not his sisters here with us?' And they took offence at him. And Jesus said to them, 'A prophet is not without honour, except in his own country, and among his own kin, and in his own house.' And he could do no mighty work there, except that he laid his hands upon a few sick people and healed them. And he marvelled because of their unbelief (Mark 6.1–6).

This Gospel is intended to draw our attention to the 'scandal' that faith may undergo if the messenger and the message of faith are too ordinary and commonplace. The scandal described here, transforming belief into unbelief, arises from the expectation that the message and the messenger, if they are to be credible, must not be part of the situation of the hearers (not from their 'home town'): they must give us, not an interpretation of life which leaves us in our present existence with its cares and ordinariness, but one which breaks through this situation and plants us in another world. Here is food for thought.

Mark assumes here that we know what is the message for which Jesus in his sermon in the synagogue requires faith. He also assumes that Jesus' claim is not simply groundless and that the acceptance of this message is not the result of a mere whim, but is based on reasons. But the passage is meant to show that precisely under these conditions this faith is a perilous decision, because it can have its final justification, its proper 'light', only in itself. And one of the most serious of these dangers is mentioned here. This danger can be overwhelming when faith is refused; it can also become effective when the preacher, the Church herself in her proclamation, tries to meet the danger by trying to deflect or conceal the offensiveness of the message itself, as the commonplace to be set up in the midst of our own existence, giving to it a halo of false otherworldiness which true faith in the message simply does not expect.

What Jesus' audience in the church of his home town is saying is something like this (to adopt the words of a German Protestant exegete): 'What's this joiner from our village doing, talking to us in the name of God?' What is the point of this reproach? Evidently the thought behind it is this: Someone who comes from among ourselves speaks in the light of our reality, of the existing facts of our life and of our ways of thought, and naturally his message cannot come from God and therefore he has no right to demand faith. For what belongs to us we already know ourselves and we know too that what we know, what is ours, has not and cannot have anything to do with God: either it carries with it its own authorization and has no need of further substantiation by an appeal to God, or it is something hideous on which no authorization from God can throw further light; what comes from us, what is set up in our midst and yet seeks to be more than we are, can only be ideology and as such superfluous. This is the way that unbelief is expressed when the message of faith is set up in the midst of our ordinary life.

And yet it is just this faith which thus rises in the midst of our life. For what does this faith say? What does it bring? To be exact, it does not add to our life a new dimension of heavenly realities from outside, it does not surmount our mundane reality, still less does it abolish this life in its dull ordinariness, with its slight happiness and its many tears, with its successes and disappointments. It puts squarely before us only the deep roots of this life which we would otherwise overlook or shut out: faith proclaims the radical character of freedom, of responsibility, of love, hope, guilt, forgiveness, and the ultimate ground of their radicalness it calls God. It is God who has always established himself within this life as its ultimate depth. But this divine rootedness is that of our life in the concrete: that is, of our relationship with our neighbour, of our miserable daily duties, of our capacity for forgiveness, of our acceptance of life's dark disappointments, of our resignation in face of death. We might say that this is the radicalness of our home town. And when this appears in the message of faith, we are tempted to say: 'Can anything good come out of Nazareth? Isn't this the joiner suddenly beginning to talk about the absolute dignity of life instead of going on about his boards and nails?' In the words of the Gospel, we are shocked and scandalized.

Instead of letting the incomprehensible dignity of ordinary life speak for itself, we prefer to listen to the solemn and sacral cadences of preachers in full uniform (we are in fact doing so now). This is not objectionable in itself. The solemn presentation may be necessary, appropriate and even beautiful, *if* we don't forget that what is said in this way – if it is really the message of faith that is to be preached – can be nothing but the strengthening (as through a loudspeaker) of the message which is meant to penetrate from the innermost centre of our ordinary life to the ear of our freedom of decision. It may be useful if, at the same time, we are aware that the message so proclaimed, so officially and sacrally preached, is the word springing up from the roots of our own existence. It is right as long as we don't fail to hear the word when we perceive it with all its radical claims only through the preaching of the ordinary secular routine of daily life.

If we don't hear it in this way, then we have heard only words of an ideological superstructure which cannot be maintained. And if we don't hear it also in church, then sooner or later life's innermost voice will no longer be heard. And if it becomes audible at a rare moment, if the messenger of faith himself stands up and speaks with a loud voice in the market place of our life, then we shall say: 'Is that not the joiner? What can he tell me that I don't already know or that is not empty talk?'

At the beginning of these reflections I said that there is something like a responsibility of faith when our conscience is aware of truth. We cannot talk about this now. But it has also been said that the threat to faith which we considered, which arises through its ordinariness, may also succeed by our introducing in the wrong place and at the wrong moment an authorization of faith which in the very last resort can be experienced only in the activity of faith itself. A little maliciously, we might say that this alleviation of the burden of faith by a premature glorification in the wrong place begins to some extent even in this passage of the Gospel. We do indeed read – and this decidedly fits into the context – that Jesus was not able to do any miracles in Nazareth. But, as if a little confused and startled by this radical statement, the evangelist adds: '... except that he laid his hands upon a few sick people and healed them.' We almost get the impression that this very text is meant to show how difficult is the thing that it demands of us.

Shall we be able to hear the radical claim raised by the voice from the ultimate depth of our existence? At least when it is interpreted by the preacher in the market place of our life? Shall we hear the voice so interpreted as the true word of God himself? As the word that Jesus himself spoke first and last, not through words, but through his life and death? We are now proclaiming his death: that is, the summing up of the truth of our life, the concentrated ordinariness of our existence. Shall we also listen in faith to what we proclaim?

MAN'S POSSIBILITIES AND GOD'S

And Jesus looked around and said to his disciples, 'How hard it will be for those who have riches to enter the kingdom of God!' And the disciples were amazed at his words. But Jesus said them again, 'Children, how hard it is for those who trust in riches to enter the kingdom of God! It is easier for a camel to go through the eye of a needle than for a rich man to enter the kingdom of God.' And they were exceedingly astonished, and said to him, 'Then who can be saved?' Jesus looked at them and said, 'With men it is impossible, but not with God; for all things are possible with God' (Mark 10.23–7).

When we compare these verses, we observe how Jesus, generalizing from the example of the rich who are unfit for the kingdom of God, is shocked at man's incapacity to enter the kingdom at all. Nowhere is this possibility open to man from his own resources, nowhere. Wealth is an impediment. But the impediment is evidently not removed simply by becoming poor. Otherwise it might be said that it is possible with poverty. But Jesus says that it is absolutely impossible for men. Is the censured Peter or the censuring Paul more within the kingdom, living more, in the freedom of love, with God who is no longer this or that but everything in absorbing incomprehensibility?

If we understood who *we* are, who God is, what we are doing and what is really necessary for us to be free (first of all from ourselves, for otherwise there is no kingdom of God), then we should hear Jesus' words, 'With men it is impossible, but not with God; for all things are possible with God', not immediately as a calm and comforting assurance, but first of all as the desperate cry of someone unable to break away from himself and from his finiteness, internal and external, out of the prison of his egoism, of narrow-mindedness, of freedom, of calm contentment with this finiteness. And if God and his power are seen in this desperate cry, the despair is not removed or softened, but brought back to its roots. For only then are we really aware that the power of freedom is present in the midst of our prison, but we are not at all willing to liberate ourselves.

This power – which is called God and is felt as a contradiction

of ourselves – judges us, because we really don't want the kingdom
of God at all: we always want some *thing*, riches or poverty,
protest or repose; but we do not want God, in order to select some
particular object only in virtue of *his* freedom, so that it is assigned
to us as our mission to be carried out boldly and with the freedom
of love, without guile, courageously, and without a formal ideology
which falsely elevates a particular, limited reality into God's
kingdom itself. In the abstract we agree to all this. But each must
discover for himself the concrete form of it which is his own.

When we hear this desperate cry of Jesus, hear it without
stopping our ears, shall we be shocked like the disciples and ask:
'Then who can be saved?' We cannot live continually with this
horror. But we have the courage (and this too is grace) at least
sometimes to let the horror touch us.

At this time we are celebrating the death of the Lord, receiving
the body that was given for us. But when this death is present
among us, we are under the law of the moment at which someone
cried, 'My God, why hast thou forsaken me?', and thus in death
too uttered his desperate cry: 'With men it is impossible.' If we
really hear both, we may bring together two other utterances and
let him to say to us: 'All things are possible with God' and 'Father,
into thy hands I commit my spirit.'

SHREWD STEWARDS OF LIFE

Jesus also said to the disciples, 'There was a rich man who had a steward, and charges were brought to him that this man was wasting his goods. And he called him and said to him, "What is this that I hear about you? Turn in the account of your stewardship, for you can no longer be a steward." And the steward said to himself, "What shall I do, since my master is taking the stewardship away from me? I am not strong enough to dig, and I am ashamed to beg. I have decided what to do, so that people may receive me into their houses when I am put out of the stewardship." So, summoning his master's debtors one by one, he said to the first, "How much do you owe my master?" He said, "A hundred measures of oil." And he said to him, "Take your bill, and sit down quickly and write fifty." Then he said to another, "And how much do you owe?" He said, "A hundred measures of wheat." He said to him, "Take your bill, and write eighty." The master commended the dishonest steward for his prudence; for the sons of this world are wiser in their own generation than the sons of light. And I tell you, make friends for yourselves by means of unrighteous mammon, so that when it fails they may receive you into the eternal habitations' (Luke 16.1–9).

People have always been puzzled by this strange parable in which Jesus at least apparently presents a mean trick as an example for Christians. The parable is in Luke's sixteenth chapter, which as a whole (apart from a few verses) is concerned with the Christian's position in regard to earthly possessions. Perhaps it really deals with a swindle that was also seen clearly as such by Jesus' hearers. But this account may have sounded less offensive to the ears of his contemporaries.

It is also possible that Jesus had in mind a steward who had to administer his master's large estates in the manner of the tax-farmers of that time. These tax-farmers had to deliver a definite amount of tax to their superiors. How much they could extract from the taxpayers was their own affair. They lived on the difference between the amount of tax thus collected and the amount they had to pay themselves. And if they kept this difference slight or did without it, that was their affair and involved no loss to the person whom they ultimately served. So we may at least suppose that the steward in the parable really gave his debtors only what he could and would have put in his own pocket. However that may be, whether it is a case of a simple swindle or whether it may be taken as something less serious in the light of business practice at the time, it is the steward's shrewdness and not his more or less fraudulent practices which is set up as an example.

In order to understand fully what this parable is meant to convey, we must imagine as concretely as possible the situation and the style in which Jesus relates the parable. First of all, he simply tells the story of this crafty steward. The audience hear it and either are indignant at a shabby trick, such as they have often come across in their own lives, or (according to the milder interpretation of the steward's sly artifice) they are simply bored and ask: 'So what? That's just what people do.' In the original parable it is Jesus himself and not the steward's master who praises him. And when, after telling the story, Jesus suddenly praised the steward, even if it was only for his shrewdness, the listeners must certainly have been startled and pricked up their ears.

They began then to consider this commonplace story in a very different light. Suddenly they were confronted with someone who is in an impossible situation and gets the idea of a fresh, bold, unexpected stroke; someone who judges his situation with cool realism but nevertheless does not give up, does not try quickly to collect the debts in order to save a little money for himself; instead, he perceives a way of salvation that apparently damages himself, risks everything on one card and wins because he has the courage to lose.

Jesus looks on the world, sees life as it is, perhaps very shabby, perhaps full of trickery, but full of resolution, far-sightedness, energy, courage, creative imagination, enterprise. And, full of horror and profound sadness, he observes that the children of this world within the scheme of their lives act much more appropriately than the children of light do when they have to face the final responsibility of their lives in regard to God and their eternity. Since the last verse in this passage does not belong to the original parable, we cannot restrict its point to the right use of possessions. The meaning is rather that the children of this world at the decisive moment see the danger and the opportunity of the moment more resolutely and boldly than the children of light seize on the moment of their lives at which they have to come to terms with God and with the finality of their history.

Where then do we stand? Are we aware that we are merely stewards of a life which, in the very last resort, in its origin and end, belongs not to us but to the mystery which we call God? Do we know that we can suddenly be called away and that, at the moment of death, all that remains of our life's history is whatever can be summed up in faith, hope, love, fidelity, hopeful renunciation, unselfish actions for others? And do we understand that this final act of life, which turns us over to God, can occur at any unforeseen point of our life, suddenly coming upon us, in any apparently trivial way? Are we then true realists, not creeping away from the abysses of responsibility, of silent unselfishness, of the folly of unselfish love and fidelity? Or do we want simply to continue always in the old, customary and superficially understandable way of life until we can go on no longer simply because life no longer goes on and we ourselves are gone?

Have we the courage through losing particular things in life – some slight advantage, primitive contentment, stupid dogmatism, a childish craving for prestige – to gain in fact everything: God and eternal life? Or does such a question seem like cheap ideology, unrealistic, like childish folly long since discarded, so much so that it no longer seriously disturbs us at all? Is everything in our life embraced by the expectation that someone will suddenly say to us also, and perhaps in the midst of an apparently casual situation, 'Give an account of your stewardship!'?

Here is a person who should finally forgive, who should quietly bury the past, but does not. Here is someone who ought to have come to terms with a disappointment in his career and says he cannot, instead of admitting that he will not. Here is someone who should have dipped deeply into his pocket to aid the hungry, even though no one would have noticed it and he would not have been able to claim income-tax rebate. But he just doesn't do this: he neglects the chance of being charitable in secret and without reward even in his own eyes. Here is someone who is a perpetual opportunist in life and, as he says, consistently keeps away from any kind of trouble and thinks himself very wise for doing so. He too doesn't hear, doesn't want to hear what in fact he really does hear: 'Give an account of your stewardship!' Here is someone who thinks that honesty in business is a virtue only if it pays in the long run and that otherwise it is stupid. Here is someone who has not yet grasped, doesn't want to understand, although he really knows, that love is not merely egoism in twos. Here is someone who avoids such questions as a matter of principle, because they are disturbing and hinder the smooth running of life. All these situations, which occur unobtrusively and may be missed, are concrete expressions of what Jesus means when he says that the kingdom of God is here making its demands on us and has to be accepted, has to be worked into our life with the decisive resourcefulness and shrewdness, with the concentrated application and the boldness, which the unjust steward displays in the parable.

Certainly the examples I have listed do not cover just that situation which is mine or yours, the situation of the unique person who reads this book. But that is just the point. Those who really possess the rare wisdom of the children of light must themselves see, discover, where and how in their own lives the kingdom of God appears like a mute, intimidating question: where and how in their own lives, by way of the continually suppressed absurdity of life, the breakthrough can occur from deadly egoism into the freedom of the children of God, into love, fidelity, faith in eternal life, into hope in the midst of despair, into the ineffable which we call God; where and how the banality of life reveals its true and ultimate depth which is God. As we learn from verse 9 of Luke's sixteenth chapter, something like this can happen also through the right use of mammon, but the parable itself is meant to be understood in a more comprehensive sense of that wisdom of the true light which is God, of that prudence by which we see and act resolutely in regard to the kingdom of God, ready to change our lives for its sake.

Such a situation does not present itself every day; nevertheless it exists, since we never know in advance when and how it will occur in a concrete form. We must therefore watch and be ready. Jesus scarcely gives us any particular moral precepts and directives. And when he does so, however rigorous they are meant to be, they always indicate the concrete situation and form in which God's kingdom and God himself are accepted as grace, apart from which nothing is of final importance and which is itself everything. Jesus knows that when we recognize that we are always in a critical situation, where salvation is a matter of life or death, we find it relatively easy to do what is objectively morally right: for then we are also ready to leave much on which we had set our hearts and had not hitherto wanted to give up.

The heavenly prudence, which this parable puts before us as the main requirement of our life, always seems like folly to human nature as such. For, however much a person continues to get stuck in inescapable situations, as long as he lacks this wisdom of the cross, the renunciation which it involves must always seem to him to mean giving up what he has for the sake of what people only believe and hope for: in other words, folly. This message of Jesus therefore will find open ears and willing hearts only when his grace gives the courage of faith and hope; when an attempt is made to learn this wisdom in union with him, in union with the Crucified and with the incomprehensible 'folly' of his death: the death by which all was lost voluntarily and obediently, allowed to fall into the hands of him whom Jesus called Father, even in the merciless darkness of his dying, although in his suffering he knew him only as the Incomprehensible.

We are celebrating the Eucharist, we are proclaiming then the death of the Lord as the law of our life. In this celebration therefore we can ask for that wisdom to be granted us without which we shall lose the whole, because we obstinately and stupidly defend the particular. But in the wisdom of his death we become wise, we are liberated. The wise death, that we must die with him, has always a double aspect, because it must be died not at the end but throughout the whole of life: it is fixed in life as a single whole with its disappointment and it becomes real in apparently slight, trivial things, in which the acceptance of death in faith and hope must find concrete expression. In this Eucharist, let us have at least the courage to ask God for this wisdom. In today's Mass [the 8th Sunday after Pentecost] the Church prays: 'Lord, we are nothing without you. Teach us true wisdom and help us to do your will.'

2
Mysteries of Faith

ADVENT AS ANTIDOTE TO UTOPIA

Christianity is faith in the future, in a blessed, infinite future, which is the unveiled presence of the infinite God as our eternal life. Of course there are people for whom this future is too distant and therefore faith in it appears to be too illusory. Nevertheless the true Christian looks towards the future and he is a genuine Christian only if he loves the future more than the present, if he does not misuse God and his eternal life in order to glorify and defend a present situation. For him the present is the provisional, something to be conquered, the transitory, not his lasting home. He lives on this infinite future in his criticism of the present. If then the Christian's basic attitude is given a formal expression, it cannot be described as conservative. For he cannot regard heaven as a reward for conserving the present and at the same time consider the restlessness of time, the continual decay of every present moment, and calculated dissociation from earthly things as signs that the world and he himself are still really on the way, making these things the criterion as to whether he really wants to be on the way and whether he accepts the constant alternation of interior and exterior life as material for faith in the future still to come.

If, however, the Christian is a man of the future, by contrast with other men of the future, he is not a Utopian. Of course Christians and, perhaps, the Church too in the concrete have often been reactionary in recent centuries. Old ideas, old social orders, cultural forms, old positions in scholarship, were defended as if Christianity stood or fell with them. People therefore fought against phases of the future which came nevertheless, had to come or at least could come, and which anyway were no worse than the times to which they had been accustomed and which they then defended as something that could not be abandoned. None of this can easily be excused.

This reactionary-conservative stand did, however, imply something more: the rejection of an intramundane Utopianism. The Christian is awaiting the real future, the future that is the consummation of God's deed, of the coming of his kingdom, of his grace, not the mere fruit of intramundane history which man himself makes and controls. And therefore he cannot be a fanatic in pursuit of his own objectives in the world.

Once again, however, since the Christian was recruited too frequently from certain classes which sociologically are inevitably conservative, he was often lazy and easy-going, conservatively attached to the existing order, because he knew as a Christian that tomorrow (as also today) sin, suffering, and death, futility and decay, will rule. Formerly he certainly assumed too quickly that he knew the limits of what was possible to man in this world and that the programmes planned by others were the expression of impious pride; when he appealed to the unchangeable natural law, he too often confused its perpetual character with the time-conditioned form to which he was accustomed. Even so, the Christian is less of a public danger than the non-Christian seeking an intramundane Utopia. For the latter wants to experience the consummation of the redeeming future while he is still in this world: he must therefore force it to come, he must hate people who prevent this future, he is necessarily impatient, he cannot enjoy the present since for him it is nothing more than the raw material of the future; he is a fanatic for plans and programmes and must sacrifice the present and its human beings to these. The present has meaning for him only in so far as it contains creative possibilities for the future. A person who thinks and feels like this, who simply cannot find in a 'contemplative' way what is permanent and meaningful in the present, who can value recreation only as a means of gathering strength for work and work itself merely as drudgery for the future, such a man is a Utopian. The Christian as a man of the divinely effected advent of the eternal future cannot support him in this, although both – Christian and Utopian – are men of the future.

Now this is odd. Faith in Advent is a better presupposition even for an intramundane future than the anti-faith of the Utopian who wants to produce the definitive future himself. There are many reasons for this.

The man of Advent really has an absolutely infinite future before him, which already exists, although it has not finally reached him: he calls it God. The man of Advent believes that no one escapes *this* future, even if he lived in the Stone Age or will not himself experience the end-stage of history, the absolutely classless society of Communism. The man of the advent of God is already aware of the future within the present: he calls it grace, love, and God's Holy Spirit. He has no need therefore to sacrifice the present to the future, but for the same reason he does not need to explain the present as the permanent, as the consummation never to be surpassed. He will see intramundane recessions as signs that we have no lasting home here and will welcome all the immense advances of the intramundane future – which certainly exist – as promise and test of the eternal future of God, which they will never overtake. Someone who must not make the present or the early future into absolutes does not get attached to the present, since he does not feel that he is banished from paradise when he has to leave it; nor does he think that we necessarily have to solve economic problems with blood and tears in order to bring about that future already saturating everything here, of which no one any longer says what it really involves and why this involvement is supposed to be so blessed, although it still takes place in space and time, between birth and death.

The man of the advent of God then can meet the future with composure: he worships neither the gods of the present nor those of the future. He proceeds towards his future perhaps more slowly than the man of Utopia. And why not? He cannot and will not spare his descendants the task also of becoming aware of the finiteness and the transitoriness of this earthly life and nevertheless bearing it and plucking from the tree of this present time the fruits of eternity, which is no longer time and is offered only to those who are willing to die. It is not true then that advent-expectation of God's eternity is bound to make us lazy and rigidly conservative. In fact, only a person who believes in this advent of God can voluntarily leave this present behind; and he alone resolutely practises during his life the total renunciation of death. Someone who does not act in this way may call himself a Christian, but he is not really one. But why should someone who is so disposed, who is resigned to leaving all things, why should he find more pleasure in the present than in the future? Why should he stubbornly defend what he wants to forsake anyway, at the latest in voluntarily accepted death?

Only the man of the advent of God is down to earth. He knows that all the answers which men produce only raise new questions and that every new order carries within it the area of its own death, if only because it is finite and therefore has possibilities alongside it which it does not itself realize.

There are two Churches in the world (their frontiers do not necessarily coincide with the frontiers of religion and those of the Iron Curtain): the Church of God's Advent and the Church of man's Utopia. Some, of course, who possess the membership card of the one party belong in their innermost attitude to the other. For in the Church of the Utopians there are people who love the man of today and not only of tomorrow and acknowledge in him an absolute significance; and in the Advent Church there are people who see the Church mainly as the preacher of a 'better world' here below.

THE CROSS
THE WORLD'S SALVATION
MEDITATIONS ON GOOD FRIDAY

I

Good Friday is the day on which the Church – that is, we our-selves – proclaim the death of the Lord as our salvation. *The* death. But let us say first of all, quite deliberately, *a* death; and, before that, a dying. A dying. It was something normal in as much as everyone has to die and at every moment dying is going on in the world in almost innumerable instances; and the different instances of dying become more and more similar, the closer each one comes to death, so that when death is actually present it is no longer possible to distinguish one instance from another.

The death of which we are speaking was not entirely normal, since it was a violent death freely and sinfully decreed by others. It might indeed be said that society with all that it involves co-operated anonymously in *that* death and even in those aspects which appear to be quite normal. But we should not put everything on the same plane: not every death is the same as that of Jesus, a political-religious murder.

This death certainly has a religious cause, the opposition of the people represented by its leaders to Jesus' claim; and it has a unique depth, which is involved in the nature and self-understand-ing of Jesus. But we orthodox Christians should not settle down too quickly with this final understanding of Jesus' death; for, if we pass over the penultimate stage, there is a danger of misunder-standing the last stage of all. But this penultimate stage, in which the ultimate significance of Jesus' death is revealed, takes the form of losing his life through being murdered when he is involved in an absolute conflict with the religious-political society. To put it somewhat bitterly and cynically, we certainly cannot, as people quite often seem to do nowadays, reduce Christology to the pro-position: Jesus wore his hair long and was against the Establish-ment. But neither should we regard his death as an unpolitical affair, involving a conflict merely between religious ideologies which *a priori* have nothing to do with society as such.

This is not the time to begin to interpret the death of Jesus in the light of what is known today as 'political theology'. But this aspect of Jesus' death does compel us to ask whether we share truly and vitally the death of the Lord, whether we too can live in opposition to the maxims of a society or whether we are cowardly conformists, merely reflecting the conventional outlook. To be a nonconformist when necessary, in accordance with one's conscience, does not always involve physical danger; perhaps it does so very rarely. But what happens then is always really something of a death: a sense of solitude, of the futility of keeping faith, the uselessness of respectability. And vice versa, true nonconformity in face of the leaders of a perpetually impious and sinful society can be perceived by the fact that it is not a theatrical gesture, not a harmless game, not childish self-importance, but a readiness for activity which receives no internal or external reward, is unrecognized, and leads a man already into that silence where death dwells.

It is impossible to generalize about how the active nonconformity required from each individual coexists with the life-style and the maxims of his society. It can exist in opposition to current patterns of moral behaviour, it can imply the renunciation of a personal advantage which society and its laws would grant without question; it can grow into a fight, when necessary, against society's institutionalized injustice and lack of freedom.

At the point where this nonconformity seems hopeless, the folly and the powerlessness of the cross begins.

This is strange. Someone who begins his imitation of the Crucified with this apparently penultimate and external stage of the death of Jesus will soon observe that such imitation is a gate through which he can enter into the innermost recesses of life, into a participation in *the* death of Jesus, which redeems us for the freedom of the children of God.

II

Jesus once said, 'As you did it to one of the least of these my brethren, you did it to me' (Matt. 25.40). These words imply a mysterious identity between the Son of Man and every human being. They permit us to go from the Son of Man to any other man in order to perceive the ultimate depth of his apparently banal,

ordinary life. But they permit us also, on the other hand, to perceive something of the mystery of the Son of Man in the light of
the experience of the unfathomability of any man. We are certainly
justified in varying these words on Good Friday: Wherever you
come across someone who is dying, you find me, the one dying
on the cross.

Were we ever present where someone was dying and in such a
way that we were really alert to what was happening? Perhaps
we were, although we are glad today to banish death into the
solitude of an impersonal, efficiently run hospital where the people
whose profession it is to cope with the dying may be trusted not
to take it all too tragically. If we really are present, however help-
lessly, when a human being is dying, we are justified by this
variation on the words of Jesus in surmising what his dying and
his death were, without disputing or obscuring their radical
uniqueness and incomparability.

What is our experience at any man's death? Someone goes and
leaves behind an empty place. Whether he knows it or not – at
least if death is voluntarily accepted, something that happens more
frequently than we observe – to make a place is an act of love of
neighbour: it is done for others. The dying person makes a place
and disappears in utter powerlessness. It is really impossible to
help him.

He is radically alone; he dies *his* death, which no one takes
from him, his death which is at once wholly unique and the most
univeral event in human life, so that this solitary abandonment
yet again unites all, and each one in every death can catch sight
of his own destiny, which quickly comes upon him, for he began
to die at the very moment of his birth. And then death appears
and the deceased person is entangled in a mute, abysmal mystery.
All that we see now is an enigmatic death mask which indicates,
almost derisively, that someone was here and has gone, and we
ask ourselves what there is in this infinite mystery into which the
dead person has fallen: the emptiness of nothing or indeed precisely that ineffable, holy, judging and sheltering incomprehensibility which, helpless as we are, we call God. And we ask further,
without being able to give a firm answer, '*how* the dead person
accepted this mystery: as the one *or* the other, as what seems to
us so ambiguous.

Jesus died as we do and we shall come to understand his death only if we grasp the fact that it was the unique, incomparable and redeeming death precisely because it was the most absolutely and radically human to a degree which *we* never quite attain: we, the very ones who irresistibly fail to measure up to ourselves and thus also to the absolute radicality of death. He went to his death and accepted it also as an act of love for others, for all. He accepted death face to face with that mystery which in death is inescapable and which even for him appeared as incomprehensible ambiguity, so that he spoke both of the void created by God's abandonment of him *and* of the mystery enveloping him as of the Father into whose hands he delivered up unconditionally his life and his death.

In the light of his life, his death, and his resurrection, we have the courage to believe that he really succeeded in dying this radical death. Hence there was nothing in him that was not yielded up in utter freedom to God's incomprehensibility, without any reservations and without cherishing any illusions which might have rendered this abysmal incomprehensibility less bewildering or innocuous to a degree at which we might in the end come to terms with it. He also accepted completely just this utter unfathomability as the protecting mystery of love. He succeeded in *both*: enduring to the very last the contradiction which tore his heart and entering into a unity reconciled and reconciling. When we acknowledge what is never completely intelligible to us, the radical nature of Jesus' human death, we have acknowledged him already in his death as the Son of God. For this radical death can occur only if God makes it, like this whole man, his own reality.

III

If we want to reflect a little more on the Christian theology of death, we must first of all make the obvious remark that the familiar statements of Christian Dogmatics sound quite mythological at first hearing. Sacrifice of the cross, reconciliation with God through the blood of Jesus, suffering that offers satisfaction to the offended deity, the wrath of the holy God which falls on Jesus in our place: such expressions do sound at first like mythological statements, the meaning and truth of which can be grasped by us only with difficulty or not at all – quite apart from the fact that it is very difficult for us to understand how we can depend on another person at the very roots of our existence, as on our own inalienable decision and on God himself in his divinity, in which our freedom also remains enveloped.

We can and must interpret such formulas in the sure conviction that this well-intentioned interpretation does not lead us away either from the testimony of Scripture or from the faith of our Fathers. We are bound to strive for such an understanding, since it is only in this way that we can honour today's mystery.

First of all it is obvious that Good Friday does not mean changing the mind of an angry God who is disavowing man, but that this redeeming act itself proceeds from the pure initiative of God's holy love and is in no way effected by anything outside God.

Neither does it mean that God, in a kind of new, second approach, brings order again into his world which had been reduced to chaos in a way that was surprising and unforeseen even for God himself. From the very beginning, sin in man's history was allowed by God to enter the world only because and in so far as he knew it to be overcome by the victorious power of his absolute love. Nor is it the case that Christ's saving deed at a definite point of space and time in history somehow impaired or rendered superfluous God's free act of grace *always* and *everywhere* sustaining the *whole* dark history of mankind or man's freedom turning to God and liberated by God's grace, without which there is no salvation as consummation of freedom. Salvation and redemption are accomplished through the entire single history of all men and through all men's freedom.

What remains then of the meaning of the one cross on the unique Good Friday? The world, we might say, is sustained from the very beginning by the victorious self-communication of God always and everywhere, in the movement of a self-surpassing towards God, towards him as its consummation. Everywhere, that is, where there is not a final 'No' to put a stop to it. And even this 'No' – this is the Christian hope which cannot be reduced to theory – is constantly overcome and unmasked as powerless precisely by this God of victorious self-communication. But this very history, in which God is the innermost power of its movement and the goal of the world, has its climax at which there is revealed and made evident the direction in which it is moving, the source of its power, and the goal which sustains it and is irreversibly established within it.

This climax of history, which does not bring history to a close, but makes known its meaning and the victorious finality of its goal *within* history itself, is the cross, the death, and the resurrection of Jesus in one. Here God's 'Yes' to the world and the world's to God become historical, unambiguous, and irrevocable. Since we can always say that the goal of a movement sustains that movement itself as its secret activating force and does not merely come at the end, we can and must say that God gives himself to the world *because* of this event of the cross. For God directs towards this event the history of his self-communication to the world and man's history of freedom, both of which are sustained always and everywhere by God himself. There is a point in this movement at which God's movement towards the world reaches the latter's lowest depths: in man's death, which God accepts as his own and in which the world accepts this radical descent of God into death simultaneously as his supreme manifestation and as that which is most its own.

If we allow history to be history, a single one-track movement sustained by a goal in which the meaning of the movement itself becomes historically evident, then the message of the cross as salvation of the world loses all suspicion of mythology. In Jesus' dying and rising, salvation history, which is always and everywhere, reaches its unique climax and therefore this cross is the salvation of the world.

RISEN VICTORIOUS FROM THE TOMB
MEDITATIONS FOR THE EASTER VIGIL

I

It is Holy Saturday evening. We are looking forward to the feast of Easter. We can have a living Christian faith in the exultant proclamation of this feast only if we try to understand the content of this faith as intrinsically related to our life at the present time. This does not mean that we measure God's word by human standards, that we can believe only in what is expected and calculated in advance, but not in the all-transforming miracle. It means only that we are bound to strive so to assimilate God's word that it is really understood, even though we know that our effort to produce the necessary horizon of understanding of that word is itself called forth by God's word and must be sustained by the light of God's grace within us.

If then we want to understand what is meant by the permanent mystery of Jesus' resurrection, it is a good thing to leave out of consideration the division of man into body and soul. We are not questioning here the validity of this dualism within its limits. But if we were to make it the basis of our inquiry and assume that we could ask questions about one 'part' of man which would produce no answers about the other part, we should in fact be obstructing any understanding of the resurrection of Jesus.

'Resurrection' as it is understood here is that of an integral human being, the final state of the one person, not a revival of his biological reality or even a return to that biological life which we experience in ourselves in conditions of space and time and in its death-instinct. If resurrection means the final state of the one integral human being, then it is clear once again that we cannot *a priori* exclude our bodily nature from this state, even though it is beyond our power to understand positively *how* this bodily nature shares in the final state of the one whole person. Resurrection then implies simply the redeemed finality of the one integral human being in which his experienced plurality, in spite of its diversity and mixture of opposites, remains in itself solidly one with a unity that is not dissolved and interconnected elements that are not dispersed.

Resurrection then as a *general* term in itself implies nothing about a future for that material reality which we know as the corpse left behind, since the final, redeemed state of the one human being can also be conceived and can exist without the material elements abandoned in a kind of total change of material: these are his own only as long as they live with the life of the whole person. Therefore, resurrection in general, as the final destiny of all of us, in which we profess our faith in the Apostles' Creed, also does not imply the image of an empty, emptied grave, nor even a decision about the time-relationship between the resurrection and our continuous succession of time: that is, whether it may be conceived as supervening at the moment of each individual death or only at the very end of time. In regard to the resurrection of Jesus there may be special reasons why the later statements of the New Testament speak not only of that resurrection, but also of the empty tomb. But in any case it must be said that the mere establishing of the fact of an empty tomb is not a sufficient reason for believing in the resurrection of the person who had been buried there; it must also be said that resurrection as a general term does not necessarily imply the emptying of a grave.

We have thus reached an horizon at which it is possible to understand something of Jesus' resurrection. *Our* infinite claim to *our* finality, to the redeemed state of the one whole person, is this horizon. For we can say: 'I am, I shall be, I shall remain, I don't sink into the void of nothingness and meaninglessness, and I can't escape the enormous burden of responsibility for my life by slipping away from reality into the emptiness of having existed.' And this is equivalent to saying: 'I shall rise.'

It may certainly be the case that this absolute claim to one's own resurrection must be and is sustained itself by God's grace, which is the grace of Christ. It may be the case that this absolute claim in depth of one's own existence can be given conceptual expression as a claim precisely to *resurrection* only in confrontation with the biblical message of the resurrection. This alters nothing in the *mutual* relationship between the resurrection of Jesus and our own claim which is conditional upon it. It is possible to believe in the resurrection of Jesus because the claim to our own resurrection is alive in us, if only we understand what is meant by resurrection in general.

II

In our hope for ourselves we look for the sign in our history which authorizes us to hope: to hope, that is, for an existence with a totally human, eternal validity, for what we can call our 'resurrection'. We look hopefully for the sign which authorizes this hope. For, however much we feel obliged to hope in this way and to resist the utterly sceptical attitude which we *might* also choose to adopt in regard to our life, there is an inward threat to our hope which drives us to look for its authorization in our history. We cannot of course say that someone whom God finally rejects will succeed in taking refuge in pure nothingness. But we are in fact looking towards God for our finality and can therefore conceive what we call our eternal, totally human validity – that is, our resurrection – only as acceptance by God, from whom the sins of our life threaten to separate us.

Life commands us (in virtue of God's hidden grace) to hope for resurrection and at the very same time our sin makes it questionable. Where then, we ask, is the sign that we may and must still hope, in spite of the darkness of sin which continually produces a new sinful hopelessness?

The sign lies in the fact that a person who has entered into a radical solidarity with us and has accepted the darkness of our sinful existence is the risen one, whom God accepts in his wholeness. This sign that we have been seeking is called Jesus of Nazareth, crucified and risen. The manifestation of this sign is called Easter. The assurance that this sign of hope appears just *here* constitutes the content and singularity of Christianity. It is significant – and by no means to be taken for granted – that nowhere among mankind has anyone been bold enough to assert that a person has risen, apart from and independently of Jesus. People have venerated not only mythical figures, but also historically unmistakable persons, as wise and good, as masters of life after they were dead, but no one has ever ventured to look beyond the grave of any of these in order to say that the latter exists and lives and has become for himself and us even more powerful in his final reality than he ever was on earth.

The very fact that mankind found the absolute courage to

assert this only of Jesus provides food for thought. If, while cherishing hope for ourselves (and not in any other way), we look to Jesus, we see, not indeed that we have to believe, but certainly that we can believe. We *can* believe with that intellectual integrity which is the inner light of the supreme, free, but pregnant decisions of our life, even though it flickers and dies apart from these.

We look to Jesus: in the light certainly of the disciples' Easter experience, but to Jesus himself. In him, we then discover, is that distant reality which threatens our hope and renders it uncertain: this is sin, by which a person selfishly cuts himself off from God and his neighbour. *He* has suffered to the last roots of what constitutes our life: God's simultaneous closeness and remoteness. Looking into the devouring abyss of utter abandonment by God, he says: 'Father!'

And, together with his disciples, we have the courage to believe that this word in death penetrated to him for whom it was meant and was heard. We have courage because we do not first have to invent him, but we believe within the community of believers, and because we see that the hope we cherish for ourselves would be destroyed if we were to give up this courage of faith in the resurrection of Jesus. We certainly need not and may not emancipate ourselves from the Easter experience of the first disciples. And why should we do so, we who in fact received *their* faith transmitted to us, and thus and only thus found in history the testimony of our hope. But, while all this is true, we Christians too can say: 'We also have known him as alive in our lives and his cause lived on in us.'

It lives on precisely in the hope, which is incomprehensible even to ourselves, of the redeeming and redeemed finality of our existence, the hope which makes us singularly free from all powers of death, of sin, of disappointment, free from all that otherwise enslaves us. A person who hopes, at least at the final basic decision of his life, even if he cannot give thematic expression in words to his hope, really believes in Jesus' resurrection. Why then should we not do this expressly and celebrate Easter?

III

Anyone who has ever really celebrated the Russian Easter liturgy with the faithful or has allowed the *Exultet* of the Roman liturgy to touch his heart knows the meaning of paschal joy. It is the subjective aspect of Easter: the joy of liberation, of overcoming death, of sheer victory. It can certainly be said that, if the objective Easter event did not exist, its victory would not be effective in Easter *faith*; if, then, objective and subjective did not here form an indissoluble unity and if Easter faith is joy (what else could it be?), then Easter (understood quite subjectively and thus alone really objectively) and joy (understood as perfect) are two words for one and the same event. But if somebody says this we are deeply shocked.

Where then with us Christians, who claim to believe in Easter, is this joy which reaches its consummation at Easter? Where is the jubilation, where the unconquerable, radiant confidence? Where is the laughter, where are the tears of pure and redeemed joy? Where, among us Christians, is that spontaneous cheerfulness which is in fact characteristic of those who have overcome, who *know* that the gate to infinite future can never again be closed against us, leaving us locked in the hell of our own finiteness and futility?

It is the Christian Easter which puts Christians to the greatest test. As Nietzsche said, people should be able to see us as those who are redeemed. But I fear that we show no sign of this. How then are we to come to terms with the Easter we are celebrating? Or, better, how does Easter come to terms with us Easterless Christians?

First of all, there is no point in concealing this situation of ours with speeches that are supposed to sound inspired, like those of a loud-mouthed party secretary when the election-day draws near on which his party finally loses. If for Christians there is a way of access to the joy of Easter, then today certainly it can only be through admitting that we are not very enthusiastic (privately and ecclesially) about Easter. The Christian knows too that he cannot select at random the point at which his momentary situation is registered in Christ's life and destiny. The feeling of paschal high-spiritedness can never be a participation in the life and victory of the Lord. For he was certainly not in a paschal mood when he cried out in the darkness of his death: 'My God, why hast thou forsaken me?' The light of Easter shines only for him who has accepted and voluntarily endured to the end the darkness of Good Friday. Is it then so surprising that we don't seem particularly full of paschal joy when we are afraid of the darkness of Good Friday and don't want to accept and endure it to the end?

If we accept our darkness, if we don't explain it away either by a tortured pretence of joy or by taking the darkness for granted (as the absolute sceptic tries to do), then in a sense we experience the empty form of Christian joy, the longing for joy, the desire for it, and therefore the readiness to accept it whenever it is disposed to come upon us, in whatever form, in whatever measure. If we admit our arid joylessness, if we don't try to numb it with drugs – which a despairing person is ready to accept only too lightly in the most varied forms – then a first experience of joy does indeed come upon us, a sense of Easter.

This sounds very abstract. We have to try to give up endless reflection and to put into practice what has been said. For example, we can forget our own joylessness and try to create a little joy for others. If we succeed, it might mean becoming even more acutely conscious of our own joyless state. But for that very reason the otherwise dead joylessness nevertheless comes to life. And in this lively pain we begin to suspect what paschal joy might be and we wait patiently until God puts it into our heart as his gift, as that which alone enables us to rejoice with the joy that is identical with Easter.

EASTER

On Easter Day and in a celebration proclaiming the death of the Lord and extolling his resurrection, the preacher can only do just that: bear witness to this resurrection. In this connection, bearing witness means acknowledging the reality as independent of my thinking *and* at the same time accepting it as the firm basis of my own life. Obviously only a very little can be said about this basic reality and truth of Christianity, when the sermon has to be so short.

We are professing our faith in Christ's resurrection and celebrating it. To make it present in our lives in this way does not mean that the crucified and dead Christ has returned to this earthly sphere of experience, to this earthly world and history. It means the very opposite. The empty tomb, attested by the earliest tradition, is not the starting point but an elucidation of the Easter faith, if only because, considered in itself, it does not imply any resurrection and in principle has nothing to do with resurrection as the final salvation of the whole man from the fate of his former materiality. Jesus' resurrection means that in the concrete he is the one who, through and in God, is eternally redeemed.

If we understood *what* is truly and exactly the 'cause' of Jesus and *if* we grasped the fact that this cause cannot be separated from his person, then we could also say: Jesus' resurrection means that his cause is not finished with. But, since for the most part we don't consider and recognize this double 'if', a formula of this kind is worse than misleading. Nevertheless, Jesus' resurrection does not mean that we ought to try to visualize his bodily condition, that we ought to localize the risen Christ within the sphere of our experience, that we ought to think of successive duration as the continuation of *our* time after death, and so on.

If that were possible, he would not have risen to the final consummation with God, but would have been revived merely for our biological life which is subject to death. If God is the absolute mystery, then our final consummation into this mystery is likewise beyond our understanding. Jesus' resurrection simply means that this man Jesus, whom we cannot split up into body and soul each with its different destiny, is the definitive person, the one received by God into eternal bliss, the one whose history does not fade in the empty nothingness of the past, but has its end in the final consummation.

Are we bold enough to believe in the resurrection? Or do we regard it on Easter Day as merely a myth and leave it at that or try to find a new interpretation? Why do we believe? Why can we be intellectually sincere in our belief? We can. It is a question of course of affirming in *faith* and not compelling assent in a rationalistic fashion. We can be intellectually sincere in our faith in Jesus' resurrection even if we have not entered into all the problems of modern exegesis in regard to this question.

Why? We can ask in turn: Can I be intellectually sincere in believing in my *own* 'resurrection'? That is, may I base my life on the assumption that what constitutes that life – freedom, responsibility, love – has a final significance and does not disappear into the abyss of futile nothingness? But if I do build on this and at the same time know that I cannot break up into two heterogeneous realities called matter and mind, which have wholly distinct and separate fates, then I believe in my resurrection. For I cannot and must not split up the mental-corporeal unity of my life and ascribe a different fate to each of the two parts thus formed. I, the concrete human being, believe in my finality and consequently in my resurrection, and what I mean by this resurrection is precisely that finality, without attempting to describe it in the inadequate terms drawn from experience of the present world. Even someone who has thought it all out and says he thinks that death is the end of everything, but at the same time displays in his life an absolute respect for human dignity, affirms in practice what he denies in theory: that is, precisely his 'resurrection'. If this is his situation what reason could there be for denying the resurrection of Jesus?

Even if I am sceptical in regard to *myself*, considering myself a pretty worthless specimen among the enormous numbers of people, not venturing to think it would be easy to find anything of eternal worth in myself, this is not the case when I look at Jesus. When I consider his life and his death, am I not bound to admit that *he* – if anyone – is wholly and really of eternal worth? He it is who really loved unselfishly and voluntarily accepted the horror of this life up to the point of being forsaken by God in death.

And have not innumerable people, beginning with his disciples, professed their faith in this resurrection of his? Was not this the disciples' experience, in spite of their own mistrust? At the same time, I think I may say that we too can have this experience of the permanently real validity of Jesus, if we seek with mind and heart that human being for whom death is victory, if we take that person absolutely seriously without reducing him to a mere idea. We do not thereby become independent of the testimony of the first disciples, since it is only through their testimony that we know by name and in his history the person whom we discover in this way.

If we were not to believe in Jesus' resurrection, although the explicit testimony of all Christendom has reached our ears and hearts, could we then still seriously say that we were hoping in faith for *our own* resurrection? At the point where we stand, we who have encountered Christianity, faith in Jesus' resurrection and hope in our own, have become *one* reality, the elements of which are mutually dependent.

When shortly we profess our faith in the fact that 'he rose from the dead' and declare, 'I look forward to the resurrection of the dead', we are really professing in *one* article of faith our belief in the *one* reality, the beginning and manifestation of which took place for us in Jesus, which lays hold on us and reaches its end in the future consummation of world-history: the redeemed, transfigured finality of the *one* world in mind and matter. The celebration we are now beginning is a profession of faith in this consummation and its anticipation in the form of a sacred sign.

The Lord is truly risen.

FEAR OF THE SPIRIT
THOUGHTS FOR PENTECOST

We are told in the Acts of the Apostles (19.1–2) that Paul found some disciples at Ephesus and asked them: 'Did you receive the Holy Spirit when you believed?' They answered: 'We have never even heard of the Holy Spirit.'

Many Christians today, if they were faced with the same question, ought really to answer: 'We were told about the Holy Spirit in our religious instruction at school, we were baptized and confirmed, but that's about all we've had to do with the Holy Spirit; we've not yet seen any trace of him in our lives.' In fact, in this age of technology, of rationally planned leadership of men, of mass media, of rational psychology and depth psychology, it isn't easy for a person today to discover within the field of his experience anything he might venture to call the efficacy of the Holy Spirit. There seems to be no scope for anything that is not secular within a 'system' of intramundane causes and effects, without exit or entrance.

If we want to get rid of the impression of a secular world, in which there is nothing like a Holy Spirit, then we shall have to stop looking for him only under explicitly religious labels of the kind to which our religious training has accustomed us. If we look out for inner freedom in which a person, regardless of himself, remains faithful to the dictate of his conscience; if someone succeeds, without knowing how, in really breaking out of the prison of his egoism; if someone not only gets his pleasures and delights, but possesses that joy which knows no limit; if someone with mute resignation allows death to take him and at the same time entrusts himself to an ultimate mystery in which he believes as unity, meaning and love: when these things happen, what we Christians call the Holy Spirit is at work, precisely because in these and similar experiences what is involved is not a controllable and definable factor of the world of our experience. The Spirit is at work precisely because this world of experience is delivered up to its incomprehensible ground, to its innermost centre which is no longer its very own.

We Christians least of all need to think of this nameless Holy Spirit, 'poured out upon all flesh,' as locked up within the walls of the Church. Rather do we form the Church as the community of those who confess explicitly in historical and social forms that God loved the world (not merely us Christians) and made his Spirit the innermost dynamic principle of the world, through whom everyone finds God as his absolute future, as long as he does not cut himself off from God through the deep-rooted sin of a whole life. If we see the gift of the Spirit to the world in this way, then it is perhaps not so difficult to find in this world the Holy Spirit in whom we profess our faith at Pentecost as our innermost mystery and even more as God's mystery.

Our faith is only theoretical

We in the Church would be able to discover and experience the Spirit of the Lord more easily and more powerfully if we were not afraid of him. He is in fact the Spirit of life, of freedom, of confidence, of hope and joy, of unity, and thus of peace. We might therefore suppose that man longs for the Holy Spirit more than anything else. But he is the Spirit who constantly breaks through all frontiers in order to make these gifts, who seeks to deliver up everything to the incomprehensibility which we call God; he is the Spirit who gives life through death.

It is not surprising that we are afraid of him. For we always want to know what we are involved in, we want to have the entries in our life's account clearly before us and to be able to add them up to a figure that we can clearly grasp. We are frightened of experiments whose outcome cannot be foreseen. We hate to be overtaxed and like to measure our duty by what we are prepared to accomplish without great efforts. We want the Spirit therefore in small doses, but he won't put up with this. We trust him only in so far as he is expressed in literary form, in law and tradition, in institutions that have proved their worth. We want him to be measured by these standards, to prove his identity as *Holy* Spirit through these, although in fact it should be the other way round.

We are afraid of the Spirit. In a word, he is too incalculable for us. We believe only in theory and not in practical life that God is infinite incomprehensibility into which the Holy Spirit wants to hurl us. We make our permanent home in what should be merely the starting point or take-off strip for this movement of man through faith, hope, and love, into the immense incomprehensibility of God.

It is no better when we give the name of Church to this country which we don't want to leave, when we forget that the Church too has validity before God and man only to the extent that she produces through word and sacrament this hope and faith and the love in which man entrusts himself unconditionally to the Holy Spirit of God.

Even in the life of the Church as such this fear of the Holy Spirit can be found.

Fear among 'traditionalists' and 'progressives'

Fear can be perceived among the 'traditionalists'. They fear risks and experiments the results of which are not known in advance. They don't want to hear any formularies of faith with which they have not been familiar from childhood onwards, as if a proposition and the Spirit which it attests were simply identical. They want to have unity in the variety of the Church in such a way that they can thoroughly understand this unity and take it under their own control. The tradition which they defend – as such rightly – is for them the land of the Fathers, now definitely acquired and only needing to be inhabited and governed, not a station on a pilgrimage, beckoning them on further, even though of course in the direction in which they had hitherto been moving. And if they admit and profess in theory the doctrine of divine unrest in the Church, known as the Holy Spirit, it is only in order really to have the right to refuse the demands of this incalculable Spirit in practical life.

On the other hand, we get the impression that those also are often afraid of the Holy Spirit who proudly call themselves or are suspected by others of being 'progressives'. For real confidence in the power of the Holy Spirit in his Church implies also the hopeful faith that he constantly prevails in this Church with his power of renewal. But why then are these 'progressives' so often irritated and impatient? How is the faith in God's Spirit constantly renewing 'the face of the earth' of the Church compatible with the peevish threat to leave the Church if she does not soon undergo a thorough change, while granting her somewhat optimistically a brief period in which to become again a home which they don't have to leave?

Don't the 'progressives' also dictate to the Holy Spirit where he has to be active? Namely, at a critical distance from the Church which is identified with office and tradition, in purely social commitment, in the will for the unity of Christians at all costs. Not, however, in worship of God, in love for a real, concretely existing neighbour, in fraternal patience and magnanimous understanding for those of his brethren who have to serve the Church in an office to which they never quite do justice (how could it be otherwise?), with good will and an open mind even towards initiatives which emerge from official sources in the Church, in an openmindedness without which, whether we admit it or not, we remain complacently and autocratically entangled in our own subjectivity. Are the 'progressives' not often afraid of the Holy Spirit when they fear death, which means here fear of the mute, unrewarded sacrifice in the service of the Church and of her mission, a sacrifice which cannot be justified in terms of a will for a merely intramundane future?

If the question is put to 'traditionalists' and 'progressives' in this way, as to whether they are not both afraid of the Spirit, the double question must not be suspected as a cheap, dialectical reconciliation of the two standpoints, nor be misused by professors and, today, by bishops who are inclined to advise a cheap 'both this and that' 'or a 'golden mean'. Of course there are appropriate middle ways, and certainly the extremes of the *terribles simplificateurs* are stupid and can lead only to disaster. Certainly among the Christian virtues are moderation, patience, and the realism which is not fanatical and does not want to turn the world too quickly into a paradise soon to become a concentration camp of universal forced happiness. But the Holy Spirit is simply not a compromise between intramundane antagonisms, not the golden mean, not the holiness of narrow-minded mediocrity. The Holy Spirit in particular must not be understood as one side of a dialectic, the other being made up of the letter, the law, the institution, rational calculation. Rather is he the one who constantly blasts open all such empirical, dialectical unities of opposites (although these have their justification) and sweeps them into the movement directed towards the incomprehensible God, who is not merely another particular factor in the world and in the counter- and interplay of its forces.

Readiness for the incalculable

If, then, all are asked if they are not afraid of the Spirit, this does not mean striving after the golden mean with the secret intention of smoothing everything out so that all remains as before and each one sticks to his opinion and attitude. The prayer to the Holy Spirit, the appeal to leave everything to him, mean rather a readiness to admit into life the incalculable, the new that becomes old, the old becoming new; it often means having no clearly worked out answer in the concrete situation, but, with a secret confidence on which adequate reflection is impossible, leaving the existing and enduring question itself to count as the answer; it means continuing, because the past provides enough reason for hope, but in fact only for hope.

The word of the Holy Spirit does not provide prescriptions which we merely need to carry out. It commands boldness, experiment, decision, which cannot be justified by general principles (the law and the letter). The word of the Holy Spirit is the question to each individual in his irreplaceable uniqueness as to whether he has the courage to venture, to experiment, to endure the opposition of the great mass (whether traditionalist or progressive); whether he trusts in something which in the last resort cannot be rationally proved, but which is of course supremely rational wisdom – that is, in the Holy Spirit.

With this courage everyone in the Church must do his own part, even though at first sight he is not in agreement with what the other does for his part. Each must do this conscious of the fact that his gift and his mission are different from the Spirit's gift to others. But if the unity of the Spirit in the variety of his gifts is to be maintained, there are in fact *many* gifts. An antagonism, a dispute, among these gifts in the Church simply cannot be avoided. For if these gifts were unambiguously and palpably already reconciled for us, there would be no need of a Holy Spirit who is of himself this unity; and, because not comprehensible and controllable by us, this unity escapes us. This duty exists for us only if we blast open what the Spirit has given us for our own – so that we do this and not something else – in the loving hope that all these gifts are one, even though we cannot see into and control this unity, even though we must bear witness to our faith in this incomprehensible unity in terms of the sort of unity that we ourselves can achieve in humility and a willingness to adapt ourselves.

But *how* this courage in regard to our own gift of the Holy Spirit *and* the will for the unity of all gifts in the Church can coexist at the same time, is in the very last resort once again not a question to be solved by the principles of systematic reasoning, but the gift of the Holy Spirit who gives himself to us in a way that does not place him under our control. We should have no fear of this Spirit, we should admit him, each of us being critical in regard to ourselves. Then the Spirit's improvisation, which we call the Church, is more likely to succeed than seeking to form the Church only according to the principles which we have taken under our own control.

MARY'S ASSUMPTION

If we read attentively the definitions of the Church's *magisterium* on the 'Immaculate Conception' and on the assumption of the Blessed Virgin into heaven – that is, on the content of the two Marian feasts – we are struck, among other things, by the fact that the Immaculate Conception is taught as a 'special privilege' of Mary; in the teaching on Mary's assumption there is at least no explicit emphasis on anything unusual about this assumption. It is in fact quite conceivable that this emphasis is lacking because the assumption does not need to be understood as a 'special privilege'.

Let us examine a little more closely the question raised by this feast. This sort of reflection is not a subtle exercise of theological ingenuity, but an aid to the appreciation of today's feast as one of hope for our own life.

The fact that our beginning and Mary's are different is not very surprising. The beginning of a life is always the beginning appointed by God to a quite particular life with a definite character, with a mission that is each time unique and with its own non-recurring history. There is necessarily a hidden correspondence between the beginning of a history and this history itself. If the history of the Blessed Virgin is that of her free conception in mind and body of the Word of God for all of us, then her beginning, which is proper to her alone, corresponds to this. But the consummation is the same for all. Certainly we bring the finality of our history into what we call in the Christian creed eternal life, and this eternal life is not a continuation of time, but the pure finality of our history in responsibility and love. But this finality comes about because God makes this existence his own. He gives himself in radical immediacy, face to face. So for Mary and for us the consummation is the same: God himself.

We cannot confess today anything in regard to her assumption more glorious than what we confess as our hope for ourselves: eternal life, which God himself wants to be for us. For the hope we have for our whole person in the unity of our existence – that single existence which we explain to ourselves as a unity of body and soul – is the resurrection of the body and eternal life. In our liturgical praise of the Blessed Virgin today we speak only of the one act of God in regard to that one person, but it is something that we likewise expect for ourselves. *Ultimately*, nothing more is said of her than what God one day, we hope, will say to us. And thus all is said.

But, someone might object, is not this consummation of her whole life known to be accomplished for her 'already now', while for us who are still imperfect and even for others who have died in Christ this consummation of bodily life is still to come? There is no doubt that we usually add instinctively to the content of today's feast the thought: for Mary already, for the rest of those who died in Christ not yet, not until the last day. But how do things really stand? We have to admit that we don't know for certain. It is salutary, however, to reflect on this very uncertainty, because this is perhaps a better way of entering into the mystery of today's feast than by simply celebrating it point by point in pious rhymes.

First of all, the definition of the Assumption of the Blessed Virgin does not forbid reflection also on the consummated beatitude of all who are finally saved, as already achieved in 'body and soul' and not merely in the soul. Nor can we say for certain that the presence of someone's corpse in the grave is a clear proof of the fact that this person has not yet found that consummation which we call bodily resurrection. Theologians are agreed, or are coming more and more to agree, that the heavenly consummation of the one whole person – that is, 'body and soul' – can be conceived as independent of the fate of his earthly-physical materiality. The body as understood in the 'resurrection of the body' which we believe is the final consummation of all who are saved, the 'heavenly body' which we receive according to Paul, is our own, even though it is not materially identical with the continually changing matter which we discard at death.

From this standpoint, then, there is no compelling reason to distinguish between the 'points of time' at which our bodily consummation and that of Mary take place. If today more than formerly we rightly stress the unity of the corporal-personal human being in the variety of his dimensions, then it is more difficult than it used to be to assign the consummation 'in regard to the soul' and that 'in regard to the body' to different points of time, with an interval of time between them. In addition, we know that the eternity of redeemed life with God, for which we hope, cannot be conceived as continuing time added on as a linear continuation to our earthly life, but is the dissolution of that time; it may be impossible to 'imagine' eternity as timeless consummation, but it is just that and not ever-continuing time. Modern physics too confirms this attitude as it becomes more and more clear how *cautiously* we have to apply our conceptual models of successive time to reality as such. In the light of this it is again difficult to say of someone who has reached perfection in his personal life that he is 'still waiting' for his bodily consummation, for in a certain sense at least it is inconceivable that the completed life of those who are finally saved and are now in the supratemporal eternity of God can be kept apart by further stretches of time from the event of consummation in death.

On the other hand, we shall also be careful to avoid premature conclusions by claiming that we know positively and certainly that what we venture to say of Mary and what we expect for all holds 'already now' for all who are fallen asleep in Christ. There are also good reasons, despite all scepticism in regard to a time factor beyond the line of death, for maintaining a difference between Mary and the rest of the redeemed. In its most basic utterance Christian faith knows of one bodily consummation which cannot be postponed to a still unreal future: the resurrection of Jesus. And in the light of this it is clear to faith that a consummation already accomplished 'in body and soul' cannot be a contradiction in itself. And the same faith takes absolutely seriously the history which still continues, embracing *all*, including Jesus Christ: that is, a story whose end remains significant also for those who themselves have already reached their consummation. And in this light a 'not yet' for those who have 'already' reached their personal consummation cannot without more ado be declared meaningless. We simply don't succeed (it is evidently impossible also in the lower dimensions of reality) in uniting in a higher synthesis and thus balancing off against each other the concepts and models of time and the concepts of eternal finality.

The pointed question we have just raised finally remains unanswered. But the very fact of raising it has revealed how close the mystery of today's feast is to our hope for ourselves. We profess our faith today in the unity of man, who is one whole. We profess our faith in the permanent validity of history as flesh and blood; we profess our hope and love for the earth, which is not merely the parade ground or theatre for our spiritual life, to be abandoned as soon as finality supervenes, and which perhaps itself, even though radically transformed, enters equally with man's spirit into the glory of the eternal God. We acknowledge the dignity of the body, which is not merely a tool to be used and thrown away, but the historical, concrete reality and revelation of the free person who is realized in it and works within it for the finality of its freedom. And this profession of faith is not expressed in ideological propositions and principles. It is a profession of faith in the historically concrete reality of a particular human being and thus can always contain more, and in more concrete form, than can be discovered by reflection on what is stated in it.

Today's feast tells us that those whom God loves are redeemed, are saved, are finally themselves; they are so with their concrete history, with their whole bodily nature in which alone a person is truly himself. He is not a 'ghost', not a 'soul', but a human being completely saved. Everything remains. We can't imagine it. Of course not. All talk about the soul in bliss, the glorified body, the glory of heaven, amount to the unvarnished, blind statement of faith: this person is not lost. He *is* what he has become, raised up in the implacable obviousness and absoluteness of the living God, raised up in the transcendent, ineffable mystery we call God.

We can't say more than this. We don't try to paint a picture, we don't imagine anything. Everything has gone through the harsh transformation which we call death. What else could we say except that death is not the last word – or rather that it is our last word, but not God's. The Church ventures to say the word about the eternal, timeless validity of Mary. Why should she not say this of her, the mother of the Lord, if, according to Scripture, Mary must be called blessed by all generations? How could the Church let the living history of this virgin and mother, the achievement of her faith, fall into the abyss of death where nothing any longer matters? The faith that we profess in regard to her, we profess as hope for ourselves in that blessed indifference of the believer for which time, Chronos, who devours his own children, belongs as Paul says to the powers which still rule and yet are already dethroned by him who died and rose again. And thus, even if there is the difference we mentioned between a 'now already' of the Blessed Virgin and the 'not yet' of the others, faith and hope have already leaped across it as a part of that 'little while' of which Jesus speaks in his farewell discourses in John.

What we say then today of Mary is really the faith we always profess for ourselves: I believe in the resurrection of the body and eternal life for myself and for all. If we seize and grasp this profession of faith, confidently letting it fall into the mystery which is God, which God is for us, then in our hope we have also understood the meaning of today's feast.

3
Faith and Prayer

THESES ON THE THEME
FAITH AND PRAYER

The following theses first emerged as guide-lines for superiors in the Society of Jesus. They were meant to create a better understanding of the religious situation of the younger generation of the members of the Order and to provide assistance suitable to their need. Since these remarks have been kept very general and allusions occur only here and there to the internal life and institutions of the Order, they may be useful also as an aid to others for a better understanding of the present time with its difficulties in faith and its need of prayer.

1. Faith can be considered either as conceptually articulated and formulated or as existentially realized. At the same time, however, these are not concepts of two different things, but of two different factors or aspects of the one faith. The relation between the two factors is not fixed once and for all and unchangeable, but varies constantly with the varying situation, age, national character, personal experience, and so on, of the individual believer. In a stable and homogeneous Christian milieu it is by no means easy to get at the difference between these two factors of reflexive knowledge. It is a different matter in a milieu hostile to faith.

The secularized and pluralistic environment with its enormous and disparate mass of ideas, ideologies, and tendencies, which can no longer be adequately synthesized and positively integrated with faith, first of all changes the situation of conceptually formulated faith. In these circumstances the difference between the two aspects of faith becomes more clearly perceptible; the desire is awakened – in fact, the necessity arises – to attach greater importance to the existential aspect of faith, to refrain from an excessively conceptually differentiated articulation of faith, and to find again the vital, original core of an existential faith. Today, when public opinion no longer exercises a stabilizing influence on faith, the whole firmness of conceptually formulated faith depends on this vital, original core.

2. The 'certainty' of faith on the part of many older people, including those who belong to a religious order, is to a large extent

the product of a homogeneous Christian milieu which existed formerly and through the habits of years produced steady psychical mechanisms. Old people therefore should not be too sure of themselves when they stress their 'solid faith', contrasting it with the uncertainty and indecision of younger people. The impossibility of having serious doubts or constantly raising questions is not necessarily and always a laudable virtue.

3. The faith of each individual, just like the collective faith of the Church, has a development of its own. It seems to run through various phases: the phase of a simple and global beginning in which very little is perceived and realized in detail; the subsequent phases of development through which a Christian, in the most favourable circumstances, slowly reaches a conceptually greater articulation of his faith, realizes more securely and deeply his existential faith, and brings together both elements of faith into a more intimate union. All this is affected by the person's all-round individual development (as child, youth, mature human being) and also positively or negatively influenced by the collective opinion of the environment. Today, at a time when people reflect more than they did in the past, a time of reflex individualism, the phases are perceived more reflexively and impartially, not only in themselves but also in their changing relationship to the collective faith of the Church; and the difference between the two aspects of the one faith is more clearly grasped. Such a distinction between the individual's faith in its particular phase on the one hand and the collective faith of the Church on the other is legitimate in itself, as long as we are ready in principle to identify ourselves more and more expressly in a forward-looking development with the faith of the whole Church.

4. The individual's faith (as *fides quae*[1] and as *fides qua*[2]) was formerly sustained by the common social milieu in which the Christian outlook prevailed everywhere as 'public opinion'. Since these supports no longer exist or are constantly growing weaker, faith today in its explicit, conceptual articulation is always in peril: it must continually resist the mentality and the public opinion of a no longer homogeneous milieu and must constantly be freshly realized and defended in a personal decision.

5. Since every man always remains dependent on his social and

cultural milieu to an extent that cannot be precisely determined, we must allow for the fact that today more Christians lapse from their faith than in former times – at least in its conceptually explicit formulation – and that this happens also in religious orders. Only with the greatest caution can we conclude that such lapses from faith are due to bad training by superiors and spiritual directors, since even a sound theology and proper training in spirituality cannot in every case overcome the influence of the unchristian milieu.

6. If we presuppose what was said in (3), if moreover we take seriously the legitimacy of a more inclusive and as such more conscious faith, then we can say that for entry into a religious order and also for the legitimate reception of ordination to the priesthood, it is necessary but at the same time sufficient for a person to believe that the unsearchable mystery which we call God is present and active in his life and is imparted to us as our goal; he must also be convinced that (a) this intimacy of God with us is indissolubly associated with and arises from a personal relationship to the Jesus who died and who was saved completely by the Father in his resurrection, and that (b) the necessary social milieu of faith takes concrete shape in the real Church and, allowing for the corresponding difference, also in a particular religious order. This suffices as long as the young person concerned does not make a firm decision rejecting directly and expressly a dogma of the Church, if he is ready for and open to a further development of his personal faith and does not make his own state and view of faith into an absolute standard for faith in general and above all for the faith of the Church.

As a result of such a voluntary open-mindedness towards a further development of his personal faith he gradually reaches a positive, explicit agreement with the collective faith of the Church: he awaits this development confidently and asks God to lead him through the Holy Spirit into all truth and so into the true understanding of the Church's faith, even though for the time being some express formulations of this ecclesial faith do not appear to him to be existentially 'assimilable'.

7. Such a further development of faith on the part of individuals (particularly of younger people) towards the expressly formulated and extremely differentiated faith of the Church demands on the

one hand a 'new' theology, which is not yet available in an adequate form but must be patiently awaited and thoroughly worked out; on the other hand, it requires also a spiritual initiation in which a person learns through spiritual experience to discover in himself what is indoctrinated in him from outside through the conceptual expression of faith.

Although the present situation in regard to faith is new, it corresponds to the inner nature of faith itself, since the latter essentially requires a full and free decision which must always be freshly realized in life; and also since faith is involved in an internal struggle, constantly in peril from 'unbelief', which does not challenge faith only from outside but is planted in man in virtue of his concupiscence and therefore of his pluralistic constitution. The recognition of such a situation is typical of the truthfulness of modern man. This situation cannot be covered up by forcing ourselves into thinking that we are 'convinced', that our faith excludes all doubt and is in no way open to question. A faith which is honest about its subjective insecurity is more secure than one which basks in an enforced, self-satisfied subjective security. This impartial assessment of faith could and ought to be allowed expression also in public attitudes in the Church and in a religious order. A faith aware of its subjective vulnerability cannot be assimilated to that deliberate doubt in matters of faith which moralists discuss and characterize as sin.

8. If someone in a religious order were to assert expressly and firmly that explicit and formal personal prayer to God is a mythological and obsolete custom, that modern man if he is honest has long grown out of it, he would be a heretic and could not remain a member of that order. This does not mean that there cannot be formal prayer apart from what can be described as 'routine prayer'. Every express reference of the course of our lives to God in faith, hope, and love, which is formally giving honour to God, is also by that very fact formal prayer. To this extent a 'routine prayer' should rather be considered as a person's preparation for referring himself expressly to God in the whole course of his life and for doing so in a situation where he can really dispose of himself as a whole and with all the existential power at his command: this is certainly not possible with all the good will in the world at every moment of a 'routine prayer'.

9. In the light of this it is easy to understand why St Ignatius of Loyola, for example, sees such a close relationship between 'self-denial' and prayer. For self-denial (that is, voluntary renunciation of an intramundane good which is positively quite appropriate to the person concerned, but which he renounces in order to serve humanity, or as a testimony of faith, or for the love of God) itself includes, although perhaps not always or necessarily expressly and formally, that self-surrender to God accomplished in faith, hope, and love, which is intended in prayer.

A surrender of this kind is accomplished existentially in such 'self-denial' more frequently than in an explicit prayer. Prayer thinks 'ideologically' what self-denial realizes 'existentially'. Hence we must understand a routine prayer mainly as preparation for this self-denial, which again implies prayer virtually or 'eminently' and even formally, if this self-denial involves an explicit reference to God. Hence, too, we conclude that, according to the teaching of St Ignatius, perfection is to be measured more by this self-denial in the service of God and man than from prayer. By stressing here the necessity of formal prayer as such, we are not denying that its basis in faith's understanding of prayer needs a long, continual, personal development.

10. In a secularized world many psychological and psycho-hygienic functions and exercises, which were formerly associated with private prayer and meditation, perhaps can and must be practised and even institutionalized in other ways apart from prayer: for example, in planning one's own work, in theological study, in pondering over psychological problems, in getting rid of aggressive tendencies, in group dynamics, and so on. Many things which were formerly achieved in fact through meditation can be achieved today by other and more effective ways and methods. This must be remembered when we try to answer the question as to how much time a religious must normally reserve for private prayer.

11. Today a really existential participation in the liturgy is rightly required, and the liturgy itself as a result of the recent reforms is much more open to this than it used to be. Hence, also, much is already accomplished today in the liturgy which at one time could be achieved only in private prayer. On the other hand, since modern man is more individualized than formerly, it seems neither appropriate nor promising to try to organize private meditation according

to the form, length of time, and time of day, with the aid of rules and regulations. Not everything that is necessary in the religious life needs to be laid down by law.

If the most intimate matters of personal life are regulated by human legislation, the result is only hypocrisy. It is wrong to assume that things which are necessary are not done unless they are ordered and regulated by an explicit human law. In this respect the orders might well be content today to return to the spirit and practice of St Ignatius, who left the regulation of private prayer simply to the individual's zeal. Within the orders the private sphere should be left with complete confidence to the individual himself. This corresponds to the nature of private and personal prayer.

We cannot ignore the fact that prayer in the last resort is not affected by the time spent on it. Long drawn out prayer does not directly and automatically increase its value and efficacy; but the period of time given to it must be considered in the light of the circumstances in each case as a more or less suitable means for that radical self-surrender to God which itself cannot be measured by the length of time it takes and does not necessarily occur even in a routine prayer. Routine prayer for a longer or shorter time *can* be a measure of zeal *or* of neglect in the spiritual life, but this standard must be very cautiously applied.

In past centuries, in a 'preconciliar' age, religious may have observed more faithfully than they do today the prescriptions in regard to prayer in the individual religious orders, but were they less egoistic than present-day religious? It is very difficult, or even impossible, to decide. Perhaps many virtues must be practised today which formerly did not exist or scarcely existed in their modern form, which were scarcely mentioned, but which today provide exercise for that self-denial without which any prayer remains superficial and are themselves already formally or virtually prayer.

12. In all this we are by no means denying the great danger to which the practice of prayer is exposed in religious orders. But this danger must be opposed with other means than imposing or inculcating afresh a legal obligation which has been proved from experience to be ineffective on its own.

13. We must work today for a more profound and precise *theology* of prayer than that which prevailed in past centuries, particularly,

even though only secondarily, in regard to prayer of petition and invocation of the saints, since these forms of prayer are regarded by many as a purely mythological relic of former times. The 'style' of prayer-formulas ought to be improved in the light of the standards set by the new theology of prayer.

14. The spiritual directors responsible for introducing people to the life of prayer should acquire and possess a knowledge of modern psychology far deeper than has hitherto been usual, particularly in regard to those mental adjustments, modes of behaviour, and that psychical 'technique' which are all, although essentially secular, preconditions for religious meditation: mental repose, power to concentrate, introspection, knowledge of psychical mechanisms, of self-deceptions, of repressions, and so on.

15. *Education for prayer* must not merely convey these conclusions of secular psychotechnics and psychohygienics. It must begin at a deeper level.

(*a*) Doctrinal instruction on prayer should be marked by an understanding of modern man's theoretical and psychological difficulties which stand in the way of prayer and should as far as possible clear these up. The possibility moreover of a personal relationship of man to the personal God, which is no longer taken for granted today, should be worked out theologically.

(*b*) Prior to any theological treatment of prayer properly so called, and before trying to bring this home to people, there should be an attempt at an initiation, an inquiry into the personal experience of an enduring, if mostly anonymous, transcendence of human existence in its wholeness (as a radical unity of grace and nature), reaching into that mystery which we call God and whose reality cannot be merely indoctrinated from outside, but is always experienced by us in our present life mysteriously, implicitly, and silently.

(*c*) The same initiation should lead modern man in a kind of holy fearlessness expressly to admit the fact that he is called by God in his absolute uniqueness and in an inalienable responsibility, and that God is not merely the cause of the world in general. He must be led to venture to address God expressly and in such a way as to give himself over completely to this God in his transcendental experience through faith, hope, and love. Prayer should not be recommended as something that is self-evident, but as a profoundly mysterious process in which man is constantly attempting to reach the summit of his life's achievement.

(*d*) Modern man may not seem to be particularly capable of prayer, but, precisely because he is no longer sustained by a socially induced apparent evidence of its possibility and meaning, he ought to be told a great deal about what was formerly covered under the heading of mystical prayer: about spiritual 'aridity', the 'night of the senses and the spirit', a more sublime 'discernment of spirits', the logic of an existential decision at the various times of an 'election' and so on. All this ought to be explained at an early stage in a theology intelligible to modern man. Spiritual directors in the religious orders undoubtedly pray well personally, but they generally seem to lack the capacity to reflect their own experience in prayer and to communicate it to others.

(*e*) There should be a clearer presentation and explanation of the situations and experiences – first of all secular and subsequently religious – which can lead to that personal prayer which is not merely a particular exercise inculcated from outside and carried out as a duty, but expressly realizes that relationship of the whole person to God which comprises his whole life in the light of God, in God, and in relation to God. These experiences leading to a prayer permeate our whole life: for example, among many other things, premonition of death, absolute responsibility in a personal decision which brings no social advantage and no praise, unconditional love of neighbour which does not bring out an equally unconditional response and for which there is no adequate reason in the other person, the impenetrability of one's own existence, and so on.

If someone is taught in a genuine initiation how not to repress these experiences but to face and accept them with incomprehensible courage, then he is already on the threshold of true prayer. His whole life, even where it is apparently secular, and his explicit prayer can mutually interpenetrate in a kind of *perichoresis*.[3] Then the 'change in God's sight' does not occur through an additional exercise leaving life unchanged, but this 'change in God's sight' itself becomes the dimension in depth of ordinary life.

(*f*) It is easier for modern man to exercise responsibility, to love his neighbour, radically to commit his own life for others, than to achieve anything directly and expressly religious. From what has just been said in (*e*), it is clear that these things do not amount to formal prayer – which undoubtedly belongs to the full reality of Christian life – unless they include an explicit reference to God; but they can certainly be regarded as an opening on to formal prayer. To say this is simply to recognize and apply the axiom that love of God and love of man together form a single theological virtue.

16. It is obviously from his union with Christ, from his participation in the life and death of the historical Jesus, that the Christian draws the courage to address God in a secularized world, in a world of the 'death of God', of the 'absence of God'. But this relationship to Jesus Christ and this sharing in his lot, which refers us to the *historical Jesus* (otherwise talk of our relationship to *Christ* would be merely another way of speaking of our relationship to God), is not as easy to acquire in an existential experience as it is supposed to be in the ordinary practice of religion. For this we need a more profound and exact theology than is generally available. According to Matt. 25, this experience is brought about by love of neighbour, since what is done to our neighbour really happens to Christ and is not merely interpreted as happening to Christ. In the light of this the connection becomes clear between our love of neighbour and our relationship to Christ, in whom and with whom the Christian ventures to address God in prayer.

TRANSLATOR'S NOTES

1 *fides quae:* 'faith which'; what is believed, the content of faith.
2 *fides qua:* 'faith with which'; faith as act or virtue with which we believe.
3 *Perichoresis:* 'The Greek word *perichoresis* is equivalent to the Latin *circumincessio*; both mean penetration. In Trinitarian theology it is necessary being-in-one-another or circumincession of the three divine Persons of the Trinity because of the single divine essence, the eternal procession of the Son from the Father and of the Spirit from the Father and (through) the Son, and the fact that the three Persons are distinguished solely by the relations of opposition between them' (Karl Rahner and Herbert Vorgrimler, *Concise Theological Dictionary*, London 1965).

ON PRAYER TODAY

This lecture was given on 6 December to the Benedictine nuns of Holy Cross Abbey, Herstelle (Weser), and has been slightly revised for publication.

From the various themes you suggested for this little conference I have chosen the question of the unity of liturgical prayer and private devotion. This is by no means the most modern or the most exciting of the themes suggested. But I think it is and always remains fresh and relevant both for life in your order and for the religious life generally.

The problem as to how we can carry out the solemn worship of the Church in such a way that both the requirements of the sacred act of worship and also the properly inner, personal and religious life of the individual are equally satisfied, has always presented questions and difficulties which are in fact mainly psychological. These difficulties are known to all of us from our life in a religious order. They always have to be mastered afresh. It is clear that no public worship can be pleasing to God unless our own heart is offered in it to the eternal God. It is also obvious that the personal prayer of a Christian, who lives in the Church and can never regard himself as an isolated individualist, must constantly flow into the Church's public worship, into the community of the eucharistic celebration, into the actualizing of that community from which we live, of the body of Christ, in which we are all united and all members.

In the light of this, there are first of all no insuperable difficulties involved in this problem, however hard it may be to unite personal and liturgical prayer in the ordinary course of things. But we are now living at a time when a new, far-reaching, epochal problem has been added to the old. If we look at it closely, we can see that this problem concerns at once liturgical *and* private devotion. And, because of this, the theme assigned to me becomes perhaps again relevant from quite a different aspect. In simple terms, we might say that we live at a time when private devotion is becoming very difficult and *therefore* also liturgical prayer. Formerly, perhaps, we had the impression that these two factors of our Christian and religious life were to some extent in competition with and against each other. This feeling is still there. For that reason, today also this more or less psychological difficulty must constantly be overcome. But nowadays both private *and* liturgical prayer are threatened by a *common* danger.

This fact makes the old problem in one way more difficult and yet in another respect easier. In face of this almost mortal danger now presenting itself liturgical prayer and private devotion are again united with one another at a much deeper level and in a more natural way; they have come together more closely in order to be able to withstand this one final mortal peril.

The danger I mean is implicit in the question raised today: Can we still pray *at all*? Is there any sense at all now in prayer? Even among Christians today there are some who think that we cannot really pray, but perhaps, at best, simply 'remember' our brothers and sisters, as we say, 'before God'. There is a tendency today to say that, if there is a God at all, he cannot really be addressed within a personal relationship as our innermost, ultimate, truest, personally approachable Thou. Even setting aside trends like what is known as 'Death of God' theology, even when such an ultimate, indescribable, inexpressible, eternal ground and gulf of all material and personal reality is acknowledged, the danger remains of getting the impression that we cannot address him, cannot in any real sense pray to him; prayer is regarded as the mythological manifestation of a human reality which essentially refers only to our neighbour.

Just as there is a danger of dissolving religion into political activity, of 'demythologizing' the relationship to God and of translating it into fellow-feeling, so of course there is also the danger that people no longer know what prayer means, that they think they can no longer do anything like this. Prayer then seems like an odd kind of introversion, a flight from life's reality and tasks. People have the impression that prayer which, as in the Our Father, presents a series of petitions to God and expects him to intervene in this world, is simply pointless, since God does not, so to speak, intervene from outside to provide for himself a place in the world, but exists as absent-present at an infinite distance as the bare horizon of all human activity and as one about whom we can at most be silent, even if he has not died in the meantime.

The trend today is very definitely towards secularization, and religious worship generally is regarded with hostility. All prayer which is transcendent in this sense is subjected to 'ideological criticism', attempting to reduce all these phenomena with the aid of psychology, depth-psychology, and so on, to the effects of man's still unmastered fear of existence and to projections which are purely man-made and thus show that he has not yet understood and liberated himself. This, I think, is the real reason for the danger facing both liturgical and private prayer. Although the difficulty has perhaps not yet (not yet, thank God) entirely succeeded in clambering over all convent walls, it is one that in some sense affects *everyone* today. Whether this feeling of being unable to address God has become explicit in the individual's personal life how this feeling of discomfort mingles and coexists with quite different religious traditions in which and from which we live, is still another question. But we should recognize quite soberly and objectively that something of this kind does affect us also today.

If we can pray nevertheless, if we like praying and regard it as something to be taken for granted in our life, if perhaps we are in fact always and everywhere with God, live in his presence, address him absolutely naturally, if we don't have the feeling that our words are swallowed up in God's silence, if we feel that we are sheltered in God, really embraced in his love: in brief, if we are nevertheless men of prayer, then, particularly in face of this radical threat to all that is explicitly religious in us, we must admit that what we live by is not obvious but is God's grace which we must cherish, preserve, and develop.

The difficulty can be overcome only if we honestly recognize it and admit too that it reveals something which we perhaps usually overlook in popular liturgical or private devotion. There are certainly two essential truths to be recognized in this danger which threatens liturgical and private prayer. And we should see these truths clearly since, properly understood, they don't destroy our religious life but only give it an ultimate depth and also a validity corresponding to our time.

The first truth behind the danger threatening us is that God is not just something alongside other things, but their ultimate, original, incomprehensible ground. Of course, if we lead a concrete, simple, natural religious life, nourished by the gospel, by Jesus' prayer, then God is an immediate, really existing, obvious reality. We say 'Thou', we say 'Our Father in heaven'. Sometimes also we think of the risen Lord too much in terms of 'God'. We speak, we pray, and we appeal, we give thanks, we present to this living Thou our wishes, our cares, and our sorrows. All this is wholly justified and true: it is the blessed-naïve obviousness of our religious life.

But there is more to it than this. Do we begin slowly to observe that this God really is not any kind of particular being, a particular, concrete Thou directly *alongside* every other thing that we know? Do we observe that God really is ineffable, incomprehensible, that he can nowhere be pinned down as it were, that he does not occupy a particular place within the co-ordinated system of our concepts and our experiences, that he always eludes our accounting for things, that we cannot manipulate him, that our prayer is never anything like a human confrontation of wills in which one finally gives way to the other? Do we observe that we possess God, so to speak, only in silent adoration of the ineffable, sacred, incomprehensible mystery? Do we see that God is present only when we spring across everything outside him, as it were, in an infinite leap? Do we observe that we can converse with God only in a divine way? Do we observe that we pray in the last resort only when we recognize this silence in which we are silenced, in which we know nothing more, in which there is spread out beneath us and around us only an endless desert and void of sheer, undifferentiated existence? When we have seen all this and have the courage to speak into this silence which seems to devour us the words 'Our Father', then only, I think, out of that which robs men today of their courage to pray, there really dawns upon us the true and final essence of prayer.

The second truth behind this secularizing tendency is the essential Christian truth that God with his grace – that is, with his most personal self-communication – is everywhere, except where the final, radical 'No' of sin, of shutting out God, is spoken. For Christianity in the last resort there is no temple, no sacral area, which is the sole and exclusive place of man's encounter with God. In the Christian vision there is ultimately no secular world as such empty of God and with an area reserved for those who want to find God in it. In the last resort there is no area set apart for worship, for explicit prayer, for mystical contemplation, in the sense that God is only there and nowhere else. God's *self-communication* is the ultimate ground even of his creation. And in what we call his universal salvific will he has already entered into all areas, into all dimensions, into all the realities of our life. Whenever we reach the ultimate truth of something – whether we are patient with our neighbour, whether we endure the incomprehensibility of life, whether we seek what is apparently most secular in scientific knowledge and technical achievement, and do this freely as human beings – this mental self-realization, even when it seems to be absolutely secular, has already broken through into God's grace.

This means in simple, straightforward terms, almost in the words of the catechism: whenever someone does his duty to his neighbour freely and responsibly, displays unselfishness, loyalty, bravery, honesty, in his regard, this is a personal, free, moral self-realization which can and must be achieved with the whole material of the world and of human tasks; it is sustained by God's supernatural grace in which, for Christ's sake, God turns to us with his own self-communication and therefore gives to everything that man does freely (except when he shuts himself off from God through sin) an ultimate finality, an ultimate inner activation and dynamism towards the life of the triune God. And this holds not only when we try deliberately and explicitly to fulfil a legal norm laid down by God or something like it. Because he is the God of gracious self-communication to the world absolutely speaking, because he has made the world at every point where it does not freely deny him his history (if this is not misunderstood in a pantheistic sense), his body, God is *everywhere* as the world's grace.

In this sense, for Christians, there really is no sacral region with its frontiers as it were the frontiers of God. In this ultimate sense, apart from the world itself as a whole, there is no house in which God dwells. This fundamental truth is a quite obvious Christian truth. In our normal religious life we don't dispute what has just been said in theory, but we act under the contrary impression. We say (and this of course is right in itself) that the sacraments are events of grace, but then we tacitly assume that there is no sort of event of God's grace apart from these sacraments. This is simply not true and it is unchristian. We say that we can address God in prayer in the Church's worship. This is true. And at the same moment we think that if we are not actually praying then we have nothing to do with God. This is heresy.

That is the second truth behind the secularizing tendency of our time, which we must grasp boldly, aware of the fact that in all this there is no threat ultimately either to private or to liturgical life, but that this life really reaches its fullness in the light of these truths. We must resolutely place ourselves on the ground of the difficulty itself, we must tackle it boldly, look it in the eyes, recognize its truth, and in the light of this begin to see clearly why private and liturgical prayer (ultimately as one) arise precisely at this point. How do private and liturgical prayer acquire their true nature precisely from these preconditions? If in fact God as the transcendent (let us call him this for the moment) is *nowhere* and if, as giving himself in self-communication to the world as a whole, he is really *everywhere*?

First of all we must recognize quite soberly and simply, in the light of ordinary life, that the deepest reality of man must be present always and everywhere, must penetrate all individual things, all that is small or great, and yet emerge as itself, become so to speak incarnate, find objective expression. Two people are united in love and are so united always and everywhere in the daily grind. And yet sometimes also they say an *explicit* word of love. They permit their innermost solidarity to come to light in a word, in a sign, in a gesture, in a look. Man can realize what is deepest within him only in his bodily nature.

Man is the one who always knows more than he can say in words and yet must attempt to stammer out the unutterable. And what occurs thus in the individual's private life exists also in the history of mankind itself as a whole. The history of the world, the history of its ideas, of its culture, all that is signified by mankind and its history is really just the history of this gracious self-communication of the absolute and transcendent God. And in this history, which as a whole (if I may put it in this way) is the body and history of God, there must necessarily be definite events in which this ultimate, almost diffusely spread divine life at the roots of all reality comes to light, materializes, is expressly stated, is manifested and takes visible shape in the word (we can now confidently say this), in the sacrament, in worship, in the community of men. This belongs to the life and nature of man. This hither and thither, polarized between the omnipresent being of the ultimate and deepest reality of man and the explicitness of this ultimate reality, is alone the whole man.

These two aspects of a human life are not simply a rigid system, but form a living relationship with a history varying with the individual's vocation, his life-history, with different epochs, and so on. But in the last resort both must always be present. And there are such events at fixed points in space and time through which the whole, universal, ubiquitous life of God in the world comes to light in such a way as also to make evident the fact that this self-utterance of God-to-the-world-always-and-everywhere has become really irrevocable and in this sense 'eschatological'. This came about in Jesus Christ, in his cross and resurrection. There God did not enter the world as it were from outside, but the innermost divine life-force which God himself willed to be in his world passed into flesh and blood history in space and time, so that now *the* sign and *the* manifestation exist to show that this self-communication of God is without repentance, that it prevails, is victorious, and will be victorious. And, without this manifestation of the reality of God-everywhere-in-the-world, without this manifestation at this particular point, we could not know nor would it be a fact that this self-utterance of God-to-the-world-always-and-everywhere is final, without repentance, victorious, has already really saved the world in its innermost reality and brought it to salvation.

In the liturgy decree of Vatican II we read: 'The liturgy is the summit toward which the activity of the Church is directed; at the same time it is the fountain from which all her power flows' (art. 10). You know of course that Vatican II elsewhere also extols the liturgy as the summit of the Christian life. Now we really don't want to mark down anything in the Council's commendation of the liturgy or dilute it with scepticism. But first of all, if we receive in the Eucharist the Lord's body and thereby the pledge of eternal life, it must also be said, not only according to the modernistic theology fashionable at present but according to the wholly normal, traditional theological teaching, that the effect of this sacrament – namely, spiritual union with God in Jesus Christ and his grace – may occasionally occur more radically at points in our life where there is *no* sacrament.

To begin with, the whole liturgy strictly as such – that is, in that which distinguishes it from other Christian activities – belongs to the dimension of the *sign*, of what in this sense is 'sacramental'; and what is signified by the sign, however intimately connected with the sign itself, nevertheless belongs to another dimension. The 'sacrament' (*sacramentum*) and the 'thing signified' by the sacrament (*res sacramenti*) are simply not identical, and it is quite possible that the 'thing' signified by the sacrament, God's self-communication, may occasionally occur at certain points in life more radically, more definitively, more victoriously, more eschatologically, than it does in the sacrament and in the liturgical cult. When a person succeeds, in a situation which God controls and we do not, in definitively giving up his whole nature unselfishly into the infinite, ineffable mystery of God, in letting himself fall into this abyss of God, which is also precisely the abyss of Jesus' death – in certain circumstances, in a radical unselfish encounter with his neighbour – this is the summit of the authentic reality mediated through the sacrament. It is quite possible that this final event, deciding our relationship with God, should occur precisely in the liturgical celebration taking place directly at the present time; but it is nowhere written down that it necessarily occurs precisely *there*. We don't know.

Granted that St Teresa of the Child Jesus certainly received Holy Communion very devoutly, the ultimate event of her life, the radical self-surrender to God, may nevertheless have occurred only when she endured the darkness of her slow death from tuberculosis, driving her almost to despair, or even perhaps when she smiled in a friendly way at the sister who could not stand her and splashed water over her in the wash-house. If we understand what it means to say that God is present with his grace, wherever we venture boldly, as long as we don't say 'No' to him, then our whole life (as *res sacramenti*) is sacred liturgy, a liturgy we have to celebrate in what may well be the wretched routine of our life. And what we rightly designate as the sphere of our life delimited, marked out, shaped, for worship, as truly liturgy, is the manifestation, the explicit and incarnate form of that hidden, mysterious liturgy which we must celebrate in the apparent secularity of life.

Since of course the specifically liturgical element as sacrament (as distinct from what it signifies, which occurs in life as a whole) is precisely the effective sign of that which constitutes the innermost ground of our existence, through God's self-communication, this liturgy naturally has a specific meaning for the Christian and is part of his life. Just as God's holy grace always existed as inner activation from the very beginning of world-history and entered into the world precisely in the incarnation of the eternal Logos, in his cross and in his death, so that, known as grace, it acquired also this flesh and blood palpability in the world, so also does our innermost deified life constantly press into the liturgy. And for that reason the liturgy, just like private prayer, which is really faced with the same difficulty (not that I want to develop this at greater length), has its irreplaceable significance in the life of a Christian.

I haven't much more time. I would like merely to draw some conclusions from what has been said and make some marginal observations. For the most part we represent the liturgy as the sacred place of God's presence, as God's temple, as the all-holiest, where we are filled with grace, in order of course to go out from there into the world to sanctify it and permeate it with grace. This is an absolutely legitimate perspective: it enables us to see the relationship between liturgy and secular activity. But I think that what we have just been trying to say provides another perspective from the opposite standpoint. This of course is really obvious to the normal, alert, and healthy Christian. But it is perhaps a good thing to state this explicitly from time to time.

What do I mean? Take someone who is depressed by the thought of God's presence in his life, because he perceives inwardly how much there is of disappointment, darkness, uncertainty and wretchedness, how he is threatened from within; he goes on to think of all the deaths in Vietnam, in Biafra, of all the injustice in the world, of all its horrible darkness. Then he thinks (this is merely an example – he could be moved by more positive considerations): Here it is really God who suffers, his grace suffers, Jesus suffers to the end of world-history; here indeed he really hangs on the cross in me, in my wretched life, in the fearfulness of this world; here he really suffers out his death. In the mind and hearing of this Christian the call continues through the whole world, even if the world is not explicitly aware of it: 'My God, my God, why hast thou forsaken me?' And out of the fearful muddle that we call world-history he hears too: 'Father, into thy hands I commit my spirit!' Thus he really experiences from within, in himself, and outside in the whole history of the world and mankind the destiny of the world as truly the destiny of God (we really can use these terms), of his self-communication, of his grace, and of Jesus – who indeed, according to Matt. 25, really exists in everyone of our brothers and sisters. If, with all this in mind, he enters into the temple-area of the liturgy and celebrates the mystery in which the death of the Lord is proclaimed, then he really learns how that which now occurs in the Eucharist is not an isolated event in a sacred place, but the event in which finally, perhaps already even in its heavenly beauty, all our life in the so-called secular world comes to its full reality.

I think, if we come as it were from God and his grace and from the divine depth and roots of the world, from a world already suffering-deified in its innermost reality, then the liturgy will no longer create or even be in *danger* of creating the impression of being some sort of ideological sphere of unreality where we take refuge and leave the world behind us: as if we had been forced to choose between facing the reality of the world and taking refuge in this ideological sphere.

Seen in this way, the liturgy is the dawning of self-awareness, the life of the most real, fearful, and wonderful reality itself made explicit in word and sign. We do not then merely go, so to speak, loaded with God's grace from the liturgy back into a godless world. We come from a world filled with God into a sphere in which what is otherwise covered up, what can be suppressed, what is not clear, what is often for that reason not radically accepted, reaches complete self-awareness.

Finally, looking at life in a particular religious order, we must add another observation. I said just now that the relationship of the explicitly cultic, of what is grasped in words, the sacral, on the one hand, and on the other the world as it were anonymously deified, is not static, but has itself a history. This relationship is apportioned by God in 'doses' (we might say) appropriate to each individual. And in the light of this we must also say that it can be the special task of certain individuals to make explicit, to capture in word and cult what every man experiences. Today (in fact, since the Reformation), we seem to cherish the odd idea that what is properly Christian has to be realized in the same way in all men. Since we think that contemplation belongs to the Christian life, we assume in virtue of an ideological fiction that at some point each individual possesses the gift in the same way. Since world-mission, world-improvement, political commitment, world-transfiguration, belong to the Christian life as such, they must be part of every Christian's life; otherwise this life is not authentic, not truly Christian, and so on. But this is really an *idée fixe* of man in his arrogance, cherishing illusions about himself. Every Christian has his own task.

And the Christian reality as such comes to be through the Church as a whole. Of course, the whole of Christian life must be present somewhere in every Christian. Even though you are contemplative Benedictines, you have a community, you have to work, you care and suffer, sharing the sorrows of the world, and so on. Obviously your life too must therefore be truly turned towards the world, and a Jesuit who goes around functioning in world-history must also pray. But, as soon as we think that the whole Christian life must be realized with the same explicitness and intensity in every life, the only result is a levelling down. Everybody wants to do everything and no one really does anything right.

In the Church and in the body of Christ each has his own particular function and his particular mission. We must all be Christians and nothing else: but this is the very reason why the individual must accomplish *his* mission in *self*-effacement and simply must not behave as if everything which is realized of Christianity in the world and in the Church has to come about with the same intensity, clarity, and vitality also in his own life. And, at a time when we no longer venture to address God himself, when he is apparently so far away from us (even though it is precisely through this distance alone that he first dawns upon us), there must indeed be people in the Church who really do this with the utmost intensity and explicitness and with radical courage for themselves and for others. We have no need to drag in the idea of explicitly giving and showing an example, and in this perhaps very problematical sense 'bearing witness', in order to understand this.

There must be people who pray, privately and liturgically, in this unity, in face of the threat which today confronts this single reality of prayer: a threat, however, which itself alone makes possible the true understanding of private and liturgical prayer. Life so characterized within an order has even today its great, radical signifiance. Whether those who pray are many or few is in the last resort a matter of indifference to the person who has this vocation. In his religious vocation he does not run after a flock, but makes a final, personal decision which he can maintain even if this sort of thing is not particularly fashionable at the present time. Then we are perhaps the very ones who can live our lives really from the innermost centre of our decision in faith. And such a life of explicit prayer, of worship, of contemplation, of renunciation, of forthright Christian behaviour, is today also a vocation that *must* exist in the Church. And if God has called us to this, then we can rejoice quite spontaneously when he calls others to something different, which must also exist as a function within the body of Christ. Each of us does what God has assigned to him and leaves the other person to go his own way; he does not feel that the other – with his mission, with his vocation, with his perhaps very secular life – threatens or denies the value of his own life; nor does the other person feel threatened in his own turn.

I want to close quite simply and say that I wish you from my heart an undismayed, natural, joyous love of your vocation, of the community of mankind in Jesus Christ, of the community of prayer, of work, of the Christian routine, as St Benedict presumably originally conceived it. I don't want to venture on the thin ice of history in interpreting St Benedict, but I think I may say that, within this community life of yours, St Benedict certainly regarded the liturgy as an absolutely obvious part of the Christian life and presumably did not investigate in a very speculative way how the individual factors of a Christian, Benedictine life are more precisely related to one another. The *whole* of our life is Christian: that is, filled with God's grace, with God's incomprehensible grace, with God's death-dealing and life-giving grace. And for that very reason there must be liturgy and private prayer in one.

PRAYER TOO IS ACTION

The following passage is taken from a letter to Dutch Carmelite nuns. They published it because they considered that it was meant in principle for all Christians. That prayer too is action, holds for all.

... Don't allow the fashions of the day to leave you confused about your vocation. Fashions come and go. And what is despised as old-fashioned today can be the fashion of tomorrow or the day after tomorrow.

It is not true that a human being, a Christian, can and should realize all at once in a single life whatever there can be of opportunities and tasks and graces within a Christian life. If someone thinks that the Christian life must be completely realized in each individual (as if everyone had to be contemplative and active, and so on), the result will only be mediocrity and ordinariness.

The Church is an organism in which all the members cannot have the same function, even though each exists for all and for the service of all. In our time we must bear witness to the fact that God, prayer, renunciation, self-denial, are not merely a smoke-screen for a secular humanism and should finally be abolished, but realities without which even love of neighbour could not be sustained for long; without these things it too would lose its radical character and eternal validity.

If, however, this testimony of the foundation of all love of neighbour is to be given in the Church, if this testimony to that which also sustains all love of neighbour is to be given in a radical way, then it requires also in the Church the contemplative life, adoration of God, the testimony of self-denial. The question therefore cannot be whether contemplation is to persist in the Church, but only how it can be realized as a special charism (perhaps of a few) in such a way that it is also a testimony for the others. In this respect some adaptations may be presumed to be possible and appropriate. But not at the expense of the radical nature of the contemplative life itself. (I know of course that 'contemplative' is a word which comes to us loaded with a weight of theory about its historical and original Greek usage; but all words carry such burdens, even those of modern theology, superficial as this often is.)

Never forget that opposition to the spirit of an age is often in truth the most up to date approach and an indispensable service to be rendered to the age. Look at some of the odd features of our time: a constantly increasing division of labour is regarded as obvious in modern society; hippies are allowed to exist; protest against the philistinism of prosperity is commended; people who live by writing poetry are taken for granted; music as a profession is taken for granted. And in the Church where God cannot and must not be reduced to man's level, in this Church are there not to be permitted any people who have made this one (not sole, but irreplaceable) vocation the main activity of their life in the Church and for others?

There must indeed be such people. They must be humble, they must know that the Spirit of God breathes where he wills and not only behind the walls of contemplative monasteries and convents; they must know that all organized and institutionalized renunciation is only practice for *that* renunciation and *that* death which is also the lot of *every* Christian.

But these contemplatives must not allow themselves to be discouraged by the cheap talk that is heard on all sides, even in the Church, today. Trust in God, grace, patience and love, will certainly be successful in preventing life from fading out in Carmel.

Action may sometimes be prayer. But prayer too is action.

4
The Message for Today

WHAT IS THE CHRISTIAN MESSAGE?

To begin with, something should be said about the urgency of this theme. The self-understanding of a religious group with missionary aims is always determined to some extent by the historical milieu in which it must exist. This milieu is changing today fundamentally and irreversibly, more profoundly than ever before in the history of Christianity. The one process of identification and dissociation in face of this radically new datum is therefore today and for a long time to come the task of Christianity in all dimensions and thus too in its profession of faith and in its theology.

Something also must be said about themes which are not to be expressly discussed in this paper. Among them (the 'abstraction' is essentially abitrary) is the relationship of kerygma and theology (in their connection and distinction), of theory and practice in their mutual dependence which traditionally has been mostly seen as only one-way. It is also assumed that the Christian message is always an *ecclesial* message which, however this relationship may be more closely defined, expresses the Church's awareness of faith.

Formal statements on the Christian message

In view of the fact that pluralism in theology is inevitable today and can never be held back, and because of the relationship between kerygma and theology, a certain 'pluralism' in proclamation is also legitimate and unavoidable. This pluralism is not simply identical with that of theology, but it cannot be avoided and is not illegitimate precisely at that point where there is a question of the necessary verbal communication (conceptual objectification) of the Christian message. Not only dogmatic textbooks but also catechisms will exhibit a considerable diversity. Nevertheless the message has a unity which is in its turn made up of many factors (which really ought to be more precisely distinguished and stated): relatedness to the preconceptual 'transcendental' experience of revelation, which comes with supernatural grace as God's self-communication; a common reference to the old formularies of faith which remain normative, even though they have to be 'translated' today and tomorrow in theology and also in kerygma, so that the language particularly of proclamation will no longer simply be that of the old formularies themselves (even less perhaps than in theology); common worship and sacramental life; common practice.

In spite of this foreseeable pluralism *sui generis* of the message and not only of theology (as scientific reflection on the message), some common, more or less formal characteristics of this future Christian message can be indicated. All such formulations of the message will differ considerably from the traditional formularies of faith (since they all have to be addressed, although in varying degrees, to a new situation). This dissociation can certainly affect concepts which a long tradition has made more or less 'sacrosanct', taboo, even though they must constantly be kept in mind in theology in its confrontation with the Church's theological past. The 'obvious' starting points for mediating the Christian message, experienced in our own historical situation (and not merely grasped conceptually), in all formulations of the message will be different from those of the past. It is, for example, not *a priori* certain that 'God' in his 'nature' and 'existence' can be taken for granted as a starting point. Nor is it obvious that all these formulations of the message should go into as much detail as they do today when catechisms and the textbooks of dogmatic and moral theology are almost equally explicit. It may well be that some or perhaps all such formulations of the message will assume and allow for the fact that a greater explicitness (which is conceivable) can only do harm to the message and its existential appropriation in faith and in works inspired by faith. (The ecumenical relevance of this possibility scarcely needs any special clarification here.)

The contents of statements of the Christian message: the necessary unity and the unity of what is necessary in these statements

Preliminary observation: However closely they may be connected, the question of *access* to the one and always necessarily enduring message of Christianity is distinct from that of its content. It is the *second* question which concerns us here, even though the approach route to an understanding and existential realization of its answer today may be very long and presumably will be followed – in its explicit, conceptual form – only by a minority of people. To the extent that the two questions are connected with each other, the whole of theology (and analogously of proclamation) can be worked out as anthropology. This need not be to the detriment of true theology, as long as man's self-understanding as expressed in anthropology is of the being who is absolutely and in all dimensions referred to the mystery which we call God and which we rightly understand (and thus understand man too) only if we do not misinterpret it as an element of man himself.

What is now to be said holds likewise with the reservation already mentioned in regard to the unity and plurality of the message; if someone wants to put it in a different way, he is at liberty to do so as long as he maintains the unity of the one Christian and ecclesial faith, the elements of which have already been indicated. Whether this condition is fulfilled in a different statement – obviously legitimate in itself – of the Christian message is for the ecclesial community itself to decide in and with the structures and offices belonging to it, through which it preserves its unity and positively accepts its pluralism as the manifestation of the riches of its unity. At the same time the Church in her earthly pilgrimage must also have the courage to say 'No' for herself – and not directly for God – and to draw the line at the point where she can no longer perceive any unity in the existing pluralism.

Presupposing all this, the *content of the Christian message* is and remains what we call in the old words the one, living, and true God. This of course must be rightly understood in an understanding that is always both sustained and also threatened in the light of the Christian tradition. By 'God' is understood:

(*a*) The absolute and permanent mystery in which the darkness and the brightness of our existence are always rooted as in that which, as the incomprehensible, the origin, the present and the absolute future, alone makes us free.

(*b*) This absolute mystery has been spoken to the whole world and to all men as the absolute *closeness* which makes God himself as transcendent ground also man's present glory and his goal. Thus creation too (as distinction of God and world) is sustained by this self-communication as grace and glory, and the world is thereby guaranteed an infinite fulfilment and liberty empowering it continually to transcend itself towards God and into God.

(*c*) God's self-communication to the world and the world's self-transcendence (Christian 'pantheism' in the unity of its two factors: 1 Cor. 15.28) appeared historically and irreversibly in the death and resurrection of Jesus of Nazareth. In the light of this fact we can grasp the meaning and justification of what classical Christology says of the incarnation of the Logos. But at the same time the relativity of these classical formulations also becomes clear and the possibility of replacing them by a translation which might overcome the shock of the 'mythological' impression which they easily create today.

(*d*) From (*a*) to (*c*) emerges both the understanding of the 'economic' Trinity (the Trinity seen in the light of the economy of salvation) and also that of the 'immanent' Trinity.

(*e*) The socially constituted community of those who believe in the absolute self-communication of God irreversibly spoken in Jesus, who hope in God as absolute future and also explicitly acknowledge him as absolutely *radical* love for man: this is what we call Church.

The necessary simple unity of the Christian message becomes immediately clear from what has been said, but it also becomes clear that these propositions are likewise necessary when we have to talk about explicit Christianity and the Church in conceptual statements and in terms of social organization.

A message open towards the future

The message, understood in this way, is not closed and finished, but open towards the future. This is not only because it proclaims devoutly the ineffable mystery as incomprehensible, but also because the experience of this mystery mediated in historical categories always continues into the more distant historical future which has its own openness, not to be destroyed by any futurology as long as man remains the being who is free. This becomes clear also from the fact that Christianity is the participation in *that* transition into the freedom of God which we call the death of Jesus: that is, precisely the acceptance of the absolutely uncontrollable, not merely in theory, but in the reality of death. In this openness the message is also the radical dissolution of each and every 'system'.

THESES ON THE PROBLEM OF REVELATION AND HISTORY

1. In the human word there is always an irremoveable duality between statement and what is stated. The word is never simply just what is stated. This holds therefore of the human word which claims to speak or to be God's word.

2. Nevertheless the relationship between statement and what is stated in the human word is each time essentially different. There is the word which does not make a statement merely 'about' something, but in which what is stated takes place, occurs, by the very fact of being stated.

3. This is always the case when human history is taking place. The word is a constitutive element within history, although here too the distinction of (1) is not removed and so 'word-event' is event in the word and not mere happening of the word purely as such: productive word and not merely production of the word. Salvation too occurs where the whole person occurs; but he does not occur in the word alone. Even the word of salvation therefore is not simply identical with the salvation-event, however much it is a constitutive element of the latter, under which and into which as its manifestation salvation itself takes place.

4. This holds particularly of that redemptive-historical act of God to man which imparts God himself to man, liberates man, forgiving and sanctifying him, to share in God's own life and glory, and makes God present historically in man's existence.

5. The word that is a constitutive element of this salvation-history, although and because it is a human word, can be word of God (and not only word about God, produced by God) only if and because it is sustained even as *heard* (a necessary condition for it to be at all) by God himself as principle of hearing and so as heard is not reduced by the creaturely assumptions of human hearing to the powerlessness of a purely human word. Traditional theology calls this principle making hearing possible the absolutely necessary grace of faith which, because of possessing this function,

must ultimately be identical with God himself, his holy Spirit.

6. Hence, in the case of God's word as it is heard, what is ultimately stated (the God who communicates himself) is a 'subjective' co-principle of the statement itself as heard. There we have the most radical case of unity between statement and what is stated, without the distinction between the two being simply removed, since without this absolute distinction in the undivided unity the creature would either be engulfed or regard itself as God.

7. This 'transcendental' element of the divine self-utterance and its being heard, which is God himself, always has its concrete 'here and now' in the historical salvation-event, to which the human word belongs as a constitutive element (categorial element of revelation).

8. This unity between the transcendental and the categorial element is not simply a static factor, but has itself a history in which it finally becomes an eschatologically irreversible unity and appears as such.

9. This history is the history of the manifestation of the divine acceptance and liberation in one of the world in its worldliness, 'world' being understood as we ourselves in the experience of our impenetrable existence and the task it sets us, together with our human and material environment. A properly circumscribed religious-sacral area in this world arises for the first time and only when the manifestation of this unity reaches its irreversible climax, when God's self-utterance and human acceptance (brought about however by the utterance itself) become plainly one and appear as such a unity. According to the Christian faith, this comes to be in Jesus of Nazareth, dead and risen.

10. In this eschatological manifestation the word has a unique function and consequently a special nature: for the eschatological manifestation of God's final self-utterance and its acceptance cannot simply be part of the secular experience of the world, but directs this world as a whole to its hoped-for, unexperienced future already breaking through in the risen Christ. But this can appear enduringly only in the *word* of promise, since it is only there, because of the transcendentally unlimited horizon which it is

always opening up with its categorial content, that the future can be present.

11. Naturally this word involves its expression: that is, the faith and the community of believers. It is productive and consequently fundamentally 'sacramental'.

EPOCHAL MUTATION OF
CHRISTIAN KEY-CONCEPTS

Concepts which refer to specifically human realities always convey more than their real content. This is really easy to understand. The free act as such (*actus humanus* in scholastic terms) is not related to some particular object, but is self-realization, self-disposal. In this sense freedom is always 'subjective' (which does not mean 'subjectivist'). This free act, as temporal–historical in man, may be necessarily extended in such a way that it does not have to be already wholly 'present' at any arbitrarily fixed moment of time.

Pure faith, hope as prior to love, love itself, are certainly not simply one and the same thing, but, seen closely, do not lie *along-side* each other as acts proceeding from a neutral, formal freedom applicable to anything and occupied with regionally diverse objects; but they are perhaps historically diverse stages and phases of the one total, basic act in which man, sustained by grace, lays himself open and surrenders himself to God's self-communication (called grace). Only in this way can it be understood that *fides formata caritate* even simply as faith is itself more than *fides informis*.[1] Faith finds in hope and love its essential perfection *as* faith and even as a starting point can exist only by carrying already within itself a tendency to the love by which it is itself perfected, by being a movement towards the consummation of the one basic act in which the subject wholly disposes of itself.

If freedom is truly 'subjective' and the subject onto-*logically* (subjectively) originally and finally one in a unity which precedes its genuine plurality and always outstrips this, there can be only *one* basic act, which in a temporal being is spread over phasic, but not mutually independent, regional objects. This conception may not be explicitly envisaged in the teaching of the Council of Trent, but it is completely compatible with this. In relation to a particular moment of a personal history, it may still have to find and reach its full nature, but the ultimate essential unity of the existential basic act cannot be dissolved.

This nature can of course be realized in the necessary transition through the world as the 'other', through which alone the subject becomes aware of itself in knowledge and action in regard to regionally (materially) diverse objects, and thus the free act acquires *a posteriori* and secondarily a regional specification; but this does not dissolve its 'subjective' nature. Hence concepts which bring out a particular phase or a particular moment in this one basic act, from the nature of the case, on each occasion always point beyond their explicit conceptual content to the basic act as a whole. For each of these phases, each of these moments, means in a way only a momentary exposure of a whole movement in which only as a whole each of these moments becomes entirely comprehensible.

This holds even of the term 'love' (*caritas justificans*), for this too is meant to designate explicitly the whole and it is so understood in the Catholic theology of justification. But this concept too has its origin in our experience of individual phases, bringing out particular aspects; if it were not so, we should have no need to add expressly that love justifies only if it proceeds from faith and hope. Nevertheless in the individual name, which remains such, the whole of the one basic act is always implied.

There are in fact many words which have this peculiar feature. For this one basic act has many phases and aspects. This remains true even though we are accustomed, in the light of scriptural usage, to emphasize three such phases as a particularly outstanding triad: faith, hope, and love. Nor need there be any doubt that this triad can be understood as representing from a particular standpoint and on the basis of a particular principle of division a really compact triad which can neither be increased nor diminished. It is not easy, however, to clear up the difficulty arising from the fact that there are nevertheless *formally two* basic realizations of man's nature (knowledge and freedom) and therefore in this absolutely ultimate basic opening out (which is also maintained in the two – and only two – trinitarian processions) only *two* ultimate *correct* basic realizations of the intellectual subject are conceivable. The dyad which can be postulated in this way certainly permits without more ado the possibility of distinguishing again in *one* of its members two aspects or phases or modes of realization, but the triad then emerging is not one with three members of equal rank. Furthermore, the traditional triple division of the formal basic realizations of the subject (for instance, the augustinian 'memory, understanding, will' or the modern 'knowledge, feeling, will') can be co-ordinated with the traditional triad (faith-hope-love) only by some use of violence.

This, however, does not alter the fact that everywhere in Scripture and Tradition there are words of this kind which evoke the whole of man's basic personal basic orientation of his activity towards God from another aspect and in the way that is best for the concrete human being in the light of his particular historical situation. This is quite clear in the concepts of conversion, metanoia, and obedience in Scripture. Others could certainly be mentioned. Traditionally contrition is also a concept of this kind, even though it too was divided into phases and factors (imperfect and perfect contrition), which however are related to one another in the way already described. In order to see this we need only ask if anyone could seriously entertain the idea that a person might be lost if he had imperfect contrition, but died before attaining to perfect contrition (or receiving the sacrament of penance). We need only recall the fact that the existential difficulty in the way of perfect contrition (perfect charity) lies precisely in that imperfect contrition which involves a resolute aversion from sin; the latter, if it is real, drives a person on with existential necessity to perfect contrition. For a subjective neutrality (no will to sin, nor any complete, subjective consent to God, as love for him) is existentially impossible (at least 'in the long run') as long as it is assumed that a totally free suspension of any decision is an existential-ontological impossibility. It is odd that both parties in the endless controversy between attritionism and contritionism[2] stubbornly ignored these simple facts.

As the history of religious ideas shows, such concepts at different epochs may have a different evocative force for the understanding and the originally genuine accomplishment of the one whole basic act of man in regard to God, and the 'key-word' which opens out to man access to the whole, through a particular door in a particular epoch, is not always the same but changes. This is not the place to ask about the reasons for this epochal mutation, should there be any doubt that the Church has a certain right of guidance in face of this transformation. She needs this right, because she must provide for the community's common profession of faith and she needs also a common vocabulary intelligible to everybody. On the other hand, history also shows that the Church does not possess an absolute power over such changes.

She has not only slowly shaped theological concepts in an historical process; in the history of her own theological thought and ideas and because of the secular mutation of concepts, she has also been subject to a history which she cannot often adequately direct nor even completely deliberately realize, but which she endures. Sin, for example, was not described simply by the same word from Augustine to Pius V (cf. DS 392 and 1925). Theologians ought to reflect much more on the fact that the later history of concepts ('person' and 'nature', for example) which cannot really be held up by the Church, in spite of all the efforts of theology to maintain the old meanings, has mortgaged these so heavily that old, formerly relatively clear propositions can be considerably obscured for the actual understanding of later times.

When someone today hears that in God there are three 'persons', he (and many others, including perhaps also learned theologians) almost necessarily takes this to mean something which has little or nothing to do with the dogma of the Trinity. This epochal obscuring of concepts, with the difficulties it creates for a real assimilation of what is meant, may certainly apply also to the 'key-concepts' under consideration here. Will modern man, for instance, easily grasp the meaning of 'contrition' as derived from *contero*, 'grind to powder', 'wear away' and so on? Nor does it always help to suggest that concepts like this should be explained. For any explanation must be based ultimately on concepts and experiences which need no further 'explanation'.

Paul meant generally by *pistis* the one whole process of becoming a Christian, justified in God's sight. But the synoptists do not understand the word in this way, as such a key-concept covering everything. At the same time it must not be forgotten that different words do not 'ultimately' mean the same in the sense that the same thing is grasped in simply the *same* way in words which are merely phonetically different; but the diverse origin of the word also implies for the whole a different existential way in which one and the same whole is concretely grasped.

Later, also, there was an epochal mutation of one particular dominant key-concept. When the meaning of 'conversion' had to be described briefly in medieval theology and piety, the word used was certainly not 'faith' but 'penance' or 'contrition'. 'Penance' may well have meant the whole radical surrender to God, but the word certainly does not directly convey the same meaning as 'metanoia' in the New Testament. Real 'contrition' is in any case an event which always involves faith: faith comes to be there or at any rate grows at this point and becomes *fides formata* – that is, a faith distinct from *fides informis*. But 'contrition', the key-word of the Middle Ages, conveys nevertheless something different, brings out another aspect of the whole, more or (according to the particular epoch) less appropriate than 'faith' for understanding the meaning of what is being considered.

Should we not look, for instance, at the question at issue in the controversy between Reformation and Tridentine theology – whether 'faith' or 'contrition inspired by charity' justifies – from this epochal standpoint? Could we not think it possible that, at the beginning of the modern age, which dawned earlier in a religious than in a philosophical sense, 'faith' conveyed to many epochally what really occurs in man's radical conversion as existentially more capable of achievement, more spontaneously and more immediately intelligibly than 'contrition' or even 'love'? Have we done full justice to this possibility when we say that faith as intellectual assent is of course the foundation and root of all justification (DS 1532), but that considerably more than this is required (DS 1526). Might not someone hearing the catchword 'faith' at the time of the Reformation have then seen the whole salvific turning to God as something intelligible and capable of being achieved, and would he not therefore almost inevitably have rejected any thought that faith is not itself *the* event of justification? All this is by no means to imply that what Trent means and says is not objectively correct. But it may perhaps help us to see more clearly the tragic misunderstanding which prevailed on both sides at the time of the Reformation.

This is in no way to suggest that people on both sides were saying exactly the same thing or that what they said was always right, that the misunderstanding prevailed only because they did not understand that it is possible to say exactly the same thing in two different nomenclatures and from two different aspects. But today, only after four hundred years of controversial theology, we have come to understand that disputed theological propositions are never simply opposed to one another as propositions of which one is only the empty, formal contradictory of the other; this was how they were understood on both sides at that time and for that

very reason also *misunderstood*. With reference to the controversy at that time, the Evangelical Christian must permit the
Catholic to ask if he is really certain that the authentic Reformation 'concern' was in no way secured in the Catholic use of terms
and could not have been made effective. Of course the controversy about this continues even today. But anyone who admits
this much is saying that the situation is different now from what
it was then.

The controversy itself has been transformed with the changing
times and has been switched into much more 'subjective' channels.
But this displacement ('Do we really mean the same thing or something radically different?') raises again the question to the
Evangelical Christian, whether he is certain that Evangelicals at
the time really *had* to leave the old Church for the sake of the
truth of the Gospel, particularly since a temporary failure on the
part of the institutional Church to understand a 'concern' might
be remedied with the exercise of patience and is not a rejection
of this concern, which alone would authorize a secession.

TRANSLATOR'S NOTES

1 *fides formata caritate*, 'faith informed by charity'; *fides informis*,
   'faith without charity'. According to traditional theology, the justified person ('in a state of grace') possesses sanctifying grace with
   the infused virtues of faith, hope, and charity. Mortal sin destroys
   this state of grace, sanctifying grace is lost and with it charity.
   But, unless there is a deliberate sin against faith, this virtue is not
   lost, but continues as a mere assent to the undeniable truth without
   charity. It is clear enough that a serious sin against one's neighbour – e.g., adultery – must involve also a waning of love for God,
   but of itself it involves no rejection of any article of faith.
2 Traditional theology distinguished between perfect contrition –
   sorrow for sin based on the love of God for his own sake, which
   justifies a person even apart from the sacrament of penance – and
   attrition or imperfect contrition – sorrow based on a lesser motive,
   even perhaps simply the fear of hell, which justifies a person only
   if accompanied by confession. Contritionism held that even attrition must spring from some slight initial love; attritionism that this
   love was not necessary. The debate is of little interest today. It
   seems psychologically impossible to turn away from sin at all without at the same time turning to God with some slight movement of
   love. And, as Rahner suggests, it is absurd to think of someone
   who has real but imperfect contrition failing to be saved only
   because he was unable to go to confession.

'SINS' AND GUILT

We don't like to hear the word 'sin' today. It sounds so old-fashioned. We feel that it places us back in our childhood days when we were expected to be good and to observe all kinds of rules which we didn't understand and about which we could do nothing except just that: be good children and obey promptly.

The word seems to suggest a God who issues commandments in order to test the quality of our obedience to his authority; it seems to be merely a common denominator for innumerable precepts which we cannot possibly observe and which we know only by studying the catechism (like a penal code) or by going through the sins listed in the preparation for confession in the prayer book. The word seems to have little in common with our experience of life: that we strive and therefore also err; that we must find *our* way, only slowly become mature (and then laugh at the stupidity of much that we once took seriously and dismiss it for good). The word (mostly used in the misleading plural: sins!) is like the governess's or pedantic schoolmaster's index finger, as they warn us not to break any of the rules in a system supervised by a strict, invisible censor (called God), who also assigns penalties for their infringement (evidently with singularly slight effect), so that everything may be in 'order'. And, on the other hand, what the mature person or one becoming mature otherwise (apart from suffering, disappointment, futility, death) experiences as the most profound incomprehensibility and absurdity, he prefers not to call 'sins', but guilt, for which there cannot really be any plural.

He is certainly aware of guilt, if he does not run away from the hideous incomprehensibility of his existence. If this really adult, mature person thinks that he cannot discover guilt in his life, then he has been granted an amazing, unmerited (even dangerous) grace which is not his by nature and which perhaps conceals from him what he really is by nature; or perhaps he represses his guilt, explains it away (psychologically, sociologically, or in one way or another). Or he has his guilt, he is still tied to it, even identical with it, and so of course has difficulty in admitting it to himself. Or he is aware of it at that depth of existence at which we and our knowledge of ourselves are still undivided, but cannot bring it home to himself as a reality when he tries to find it in the light of his mistaken idea of what is meant by sin and guilt.

Whatever the situation of individuals may be, there is such a thing as guilt. The personal experience of individuals, the testimony of the greatest interpreters of human existence, and the final interpretation given by Christian revelation (by proclaiming simply the miracle of forgiveness and really nothing else) bear witness to the reality of guilt. It is first and last not something which we, while remaining essentially good, have done at some particular point of time in our past life; but we are ourselves this guilt, when we freely say 'No' to ourselves (who are by nature directed to God), to the ultimate meaning of our existence, to the ineffable, sacred mystery in which we are unfathomably rooted, which seeks silently to speak to us as eternal love.

PEACE AS MANDATE

The theme of 'Peace as Mandate', on which I am to speak here, is so broad and so difficult that all I can really do is to make two or three fragmentary comments which are inevitably selected rather arbitrarily. The theme of peace is so immensely wide also because we can speak of a mandate only if we understand by peace something much more than the mere absence of armed conflicts between states, carried on with conventional or atomic weapons, or the absence of civil wars involving bloodshed: it must be understood in a broader sense as the 'work of justice', and therefore there is no peace in this sense wherever in the social or private sphere anyone does wrong to another. If we speak of peace as mandate, then we certainly mean also that our reflections must not be on a too abstract and theoretical doctrine, but must be aimed at concrete decisions for attitudes and actions, even though they cannot provide the individual with recipes for cooking up peace.

The question of peace should not be rendered *a priori* innocuous and thus open only to illusory answers by too hastily commending peace in an empirical and social sense as a simple, universally intelligible ideal, in regard to which the only question is *how* we can attain and maintain it. Perhaps some will say that, to be honest, they cannot regard 'eternal peace' in this world simply as an unquestionable ideal; perhaps others will say that aggression and aggressive instincts are anyway part of life and only a hypocrite or an innocent could deny this. We might again object that this nevertheless neither authorizes nor excuses the destructive madness and horror of wars as conducted in Vietnam and Biafra, as we have all only recently experienced them, and as they threaten us in still more terrifying forms; but then the further question could be raised as to how such wars, which no one claims to want, are in fact related to that violence and aggression which are everywhere present in human life and are at the root of these wars, and yet which no one, if he is honest, can claim to have conquered or perhaps even have wanted to conquer in himself.

We might also ask what really is force considered existentially-ontologically, that force which in the form of war is simply the bloody and brutal manifestation of power. We might say that force in a very abstract but nevertheless very real sense is already present wherever someone changes really or ideologically another's situation of freedom, without being previously authorized to do so by the free consent of the other person; we might say that in this sense we are continually, inevitably engaged in violent mutual oppression and simply must admit therefore that any real question in regard to force can be raised only with reference to its concrete forms and its extent.

From this standpoint it could be said that it is Utopian to assume that institutionalized injustice in society could be removed without force, in a 'peaceful' way, that everything desirable in human life could be attained in practice without violent revolution.

All these questions are mentioned not in order to be answered here, but only to show how difficult is the whole question of peace even theoretically, quite apart from all the practical problems with which peace conferences, disarmament negotiations, UNO debates, are endlessly occupied. On all these questions, in order at least to indicate a certain horizon of understanding and to give a direction to our reflections, this much may be said:

I don't think that the Christian, who alone can actually have the courage to be a sober realist (because he believes in *infinite* scope for forgiveness), can condemn *a priori* and reject as profoundly immoral in the fundamental sense indicated above every use of force. For there is in fact in human existence an inevitable, necessary force which, for that very reason, cannot *a priori* and absolutely be qualified as immoral. But this very Christian (explicitly or anonymously) as a realist knows that this force in man's concrete existence is always liable to be influenced by selfish, immoral, irreligious perversity, indeed that the concrete structures of power in man's private sphere and in society are always marked by his selfishness, hardened by this, and misused as a means of oppressing the other person. From this standpoint the Christian perceives that the Utopia of the Sermon on the Mount, including the will to seek peace at our own expense, the incomprehensible folly of love, and the renunciation of force, indicates and stubbornly demands the sense of direction and the goal which human decision and action must never abandon, if they are not to become expressly or secretly a mortally culpable assent to the actual, sinful perversity of force in the world. Since today certainly the threatening conflicts between the powers can least of all be overcome simply by smart compromises between plural egoisms, it is at this very time that the Utopia of the Sermon on the Mount, the courage to risk being fooled and cheated, the foolish wisdom of the Gospel, in the long run constitute the most realistic and promising policy, even though these maxims cannot be reduced to a single norm which would *a priori* spare us the torment and burden of historical decision.

If peace is to be our mandate, we must certainly ask ourselves what we must do in practice. If we are looking here for an answer to a concrete question, this of course does not mean that we are going to pass on the word for concrete forms of action for peace, that we shall for instance call for protest against the war in Vietnam, against dictatorship in Greece, against a police regime in Mexico, and so on. But it ought to be possible none the less to do something more constructive than merely make a protestation of our will to peace. In attempting this, we must always remember that human beings and groups of human beings, Christians and Christian groups, in virtue of the one appeal to the same dignity of man or to the Gospel, can reach opposite decisions and demands without being justified in accusing one another of betraying ultimate positions; which again does not mean that there can be no serious appeal to conscience.

What we shall attempt to say concretely therefore on our mandate to work for peace is subject to the reservation that others may perhaps be able to reject these concrete expressions of the will to peace as false or Utopian, and not really serving the cause of peace. There are in fact no concrete positions or norms which can be shared by *all*. But anyone who uses this as an excuse for not formulating any of these, who talks merely in abstract generalities, which every one approves and which hurt no one, is *a priori* ruled out of the struggle for peace.

The institutionalized injustice of our society

The first thing I want to say is that, if we want to work and struggle for peace, we must first of all learn to see the institutionalized injustices in our own society.

Injustice does not exist merely when someone, with subjective awareness, offends against the rules of the game accepted in the society to which he belongs; these rules of the game, the institutionalisms of our society, can themselves together with their legal framework be unjust. For the most part we don't see this, at least as long as this institutionalized injustice works out to our own advantage. This, however, we must learn to see in the struggle against society's prejudices, which are assumed to be obviously right, are inculcated in us from youth onwards, and apparently simply cannot be eliminated from our own self-understanding.

What housewife in our country, when she buys bananas, thinks that these are so cheap because they have been plucked somewhere in the world for starvation wages? At most she will continue to bewail the fact that bananas are so dear. Who thinks, when he buys a tufted carpet, of what wages the 'poor devil' in Persia or India received for the tufting, how much of the price paid gets back to the person who has produced it by his arduous labour, and how much remains in the hands of intermediaries, profit-hungry entrepreneurs and speculators?

Once again, we must learn to see institutionalized injustices. They are to be found everywhere; we are all beneficiaries of injustice. Not only the big capitalists and the people who are rich by European or American standards, but also the little man in our country who perhaps thinks he is exploited and is sorry for himself, whose standard of life is defended and driven higher by his party or trade union: we all live by earning from the so-called under-developed countries through our industry and exports more than we give to them for their life through imports from there and through our alms, described as development aid.

It is certainly part of the tragedy of human existence that we cannot simply and straightforwardly break out of this world where institutionalized injustices are taken for granted merely by a decision to do so, in order to become just; for a Catholic theology will at least not describe *a priori* as personal sin every participation in these conditions to one's own advantage, even though the question remains serious and urgent as to what is the exact point at which collusion with the institutionalized injustice of our sphere of life begins in practice to involve us directly and personally in guilt for which we have no answer. But even these social conditions, in which (in theological terms) the concupiscent existence of man stemming from sin and impelling to sin finds objective social expression, still leave the individual a certain scope for a personal attitude to these conditions, so that he can either simply approve and exploit them uncritically to his own advantage or critically dissociate himself from them and in principle seek to change them.

In order, however, constantly to renew this critical dissociation, we must first of all develop and strengthen our capacity to see these institutionalized injustices at all. Much in our life and in our society is less good and natural than the more or less sated citizen of the welfare state suspects or wants to admit. But only when we so critically dissociate ourselves from it, first of all at least in knowledge, in a change of awareness, do we begin to acquire the right attitude towards the roots of all wars, of all selfish and brutal violence. We cannot want peace and at the same time naïvely and selfishly identify ourselves with its causes merely because they happen for the time being to be to our advantage. In small and anonymous matters we behave just like those industrialists who call in fact for peace, but want to earn as much as possible from an increasingly stoked up armaments industry. In brief, we must first of all learn to see that we are *all* beneficiaries of unjustly structured institutions.

Temptation to take refuge in privacy

We must learn to overcome the temptation to take refuge in privacy. We often say, and certainly not unfairly, that politics is a dirty business. And Christians with a selective understanding of their Christianity and humanists cherishing the humanistic ideals of the educated middle class of the nineteenth century only too easily draw from this the conclusion that the upright and high-minded person can only flourish in a private sphere, behind walls through which the noise of politics, the ugly party strife, what we are accustomed to call the bickerings of politicians, penetrate as little as possible. But the decision on peace and war, in the broadest sense of these terms, is not taken in the private sphere of noble minds. Anyone who retires to that sphere alone has really already betrayed peace, since he will not fight for it and, as far as it does still exist, wants to enjoy it as a parasite living on those who really defend it, pledge themselves to it, and pay for it.

The Christian and the humanist today have a sociopolitical and a social-critical task, and only when they attend to this, together with their Churches and other groups, do they also take up the mission of peace which is theirs. We must be able to leave our own home, have the courage to defend a decision in public, to get involved in the business of politics, to co-operate with all institutions which help to determine social life.

The opportunities for the individual in this respect may be very different with different ages, levels of education, callings and other life-tasks, and they may also be very slight. But if opportunities seem to be rare, this does not mean that we are morally justified in neglecting even these. We need only ask how many of our people, apart from the ballot-paper, are committed in and with a party or an otherwise sociopolitically effective group in order to see that most of them think that they can retire to a private sphere, that they can remain 'neutral', trusting others to fight for the good of all, for a society which permits real peace.

Improving the political climate

If we want to work for peace, we must stand out in our own country for the improvement of the climate of the political struggle by overcoming the selfishness of parties and social groups. In my opinion, this means above all making an effort to loosen and break through the dividing lines and the fronts set up between these parties and social groups, not allowing these institutionalized groups in society to judge from our attitude that they are more attractive when they try to impress us with monolithic views and programmes, and when they think that they alone have all the truth and all the right programmes. Political parties and other social groups must certainly have a programme, they may defend this as better than the others, they may fight and propagate their ideas. But in very many and important concrete, individual questions even such fundamental positions and programmes must leave the way open for many possible decisions: for the really right and promising concrete form of social action cannot simply be deduced from these programmes and ultimate positions, but can be discovered only after arduous reflection and dialogue with as many people as possible.

If this is so, is it not odd and amazing that the opposed opinions and decisions comparatively rarely run squarely across the fronts of these groups? Does not this sort of thing create a suspicion that these decisions and opinions are not influenced by the nature of the situation, but inspired by party egoisms or manipulated by forces which remain anonymous? How little do the groups and parties respect courageous nonconformists in their own ranks? Does it ever happen that one party considers a member of the other to be more suitable for a particular office? From the nature of the case this would really be possible, since no party has at its disposal a large surplus of qualified people who are not being used. And yet the parties scarcely ever do this sort of thing. As we said, we should demonstrate by our whole attitude that we can respect a party more when it can live with its nonconformists, when it makes no attempt at a pretence of being very wise or still less omniscient, when it can also publicly admit serious mistakes.

Breaking down the fronts

The individual parties in our country have each a very firm and immovable regular body of voters, which in turn leads the parties themselves to be very immovable and self-assured. Is this a state of affairs worth striving for, or does it serve merely to cement social conditions which certainly cannot claim *a priori* to be always just and cannot always be used to build up a better future? Would not a greater mobility of the electorate, resulting from their own reflection and personal independence of thought, be more useful? Why do we regard it almost instinctively as a symptom of stupidity or moral immaturity when someone transfers from one party to another, why is such a person regarded almost as a renegade?

I think we should all work to break down the fronts between the parties, because it is only in this way that scope can be gained and preserved for really creative new plans. We should count it as greatly to the credit of *the* parties who manage to facilitate the entry of as much freedom of opinion and decision as possible, not only into secret party sessions behind more or less closed doors, but also into Parliament. Where some sort of mobility of the social groups and parties increasingly declines, the end cannot fail to be either a fatal and unfruitful rigidity of social life or a violent conflict between these rigid groups, a conflict which from the nature of the case would be a war even if it were carried on without bloodshed. Work on such a breakdown of the fronts between the formal social groups is true work for peace, particularly since peace does not mean the immobility of socially obdurate groups before a violent conflict, but scope for the possibility of creative freedom when each considers the other self-critically first of all not as a political opponent, but – at least until proof of the opposite is forthcoming – the one in whom, as distinct from oneself, the creative spark is lit for a better future.

If we want to serve peace, we must be clear about the fact that it is we ourselves through our selfishness, our irrational emotionalism, who prevent those directly responsible for social decisions and changes – that is, parties and governments – from allowing cool expertise and creative individualism to prevail and thus to serve the cause of peace. We are the people, the electorate, which governments and parties take into consideration – perhaps, in a way, must consider – which prejudice the objectively right decisions on social and foreign policy on the part of those directly responsible for these things. We often complain, for example, that the parties distribute gifts in anticipation of an election; but where are the groups among the electors who overcome their group selfishness and for their own part refuse such gifts, declaring that they should not be regarded as so politically immature as to accept such gifts, and thus make it impossible for the parties they elect to take relevant and even harsh sociopolitical decisions? It is we, the electorate, who often corrupt the parties and not the parties which corrupt us.

Examples of our responsibility

Let me elucidate our own responsibility in regard to those who are directly responsible for political decisions in the light of some examples.

Overcoming group selfishness

Would German policy – for example, in regard to the East and the German Democratic Republic – not have been more courageous, more constructive and more relevant to the concrete facts of the situation after a lost war, would it not have served better the cause of peace, if the parties had not been anxiously watching their election chances and having continually to adapt themselves to a mass of electors reacting even more short-sightedly and emotionally, with greater selfishness as a group, than the parties left to themselves would do?

Naturally, politics must be carried on with expertise and in concrete questions it is certainly often difficult to say what this expertise requires. We certainly don't want to go into these questions ourselves here, if only because we have neither the time nor the competence to deal with them. But it is certain that governments and parties could often serve peace better if they were able in conscience to assume that behind them was a genuinely and truly peaceful nation, a nation which is what we ourselves are and to which each individual makes his own contribution.

We are under the influence of a romantic idea and what is basically a cowardly illusion when we think and constantly assert that the so-called 'little man' (and in this connection we are all glad to be little men) is particularly peace-loving. The little man naturally doesn't want to join the army or go to war; he doesn't want bombs to fall on his house or to have to go hungry. But at the roots of his nature he is just as selfish, as irrational in his feelings, as other people whom he likes to regard as the wire-pullers of political struggles and wars. The small selfishnesses of the little man are gathered together and accumulated in the selfishnesses of parties and states; indeed, the question may be raised as to whether party-leaders don't often display greater expertise and sometimes even curb and dilute the group-selfishness of the masses. But in any case all that confronts us in large-scale politics is simply our own selfishness as in a mirror, only magnified a million times and therefore all the more dangerous.

Responsibility for the Third World

Another example. If today world-politics must be carried on in a world becoming increasingly one, in which each depends for better or worse on everyone else, then our approach to the hungry and under-developed peoples who make up the greater part of mankind, development aid in the most varied shapes and forms, is a central question not only for an idealistic humanitarianism, but also for our own survival in a future that is already imminent.

But what do we – the so-called peace-loving little man – what do we permit the statesmen and parties in this respect? When it occurs to us (which is not often), we read Paul VI's *Populorum Progressio*; we send a minister to New Delhi and let him deliver a benevolent address there. We let this question run through our minds and touch our hearts, but we don't let it touch our pockets. We permit our governments to give alms to other nations in order to keep our conscience clear; at the same time we are content to earn increasingly more from these nations than they receive from us to stop them from going hungry. We the little people, who think we are so peace-loving, don't really give our leaders any chance to act in a really peaceful way.

Right to conscientious objection
A further example. Do we really direct our governments to make laws which are fair to conscientious objectors and see that these are carried out? The Second Vatican Council declared: 'It seems right that laws make humane provisions for the case of those who for reasons of conscience refuse to bear arms, provided however that they accept some other form of service to the human community.' I don't think that the form of such laws and their practical application with us are such as really to correspond to the spirit of this conciliar declaration, since they do not yet commend, to quote the Council's words again, 'those who renounce the use of violence in the vindication of their rights' (*Gaudium et Spes*, 78, 79).

All these are only given as examples to show that we ourselves are often still far from being disposed and so acting as to let governments and parties not only speak of peace, but also – if necessary, at our expense – make it. Often enough we want peace, but don't want to pay for it.

When are we peace-loving?

The theologian, accustomed to preaching and having to speak here about peace as a mandate for each one of us, may be allowed once again to talk in a general way.

When are we peace-loving? A lover of peace, I think, is someone who can change his view, since it is only in this way that there can be any hope of agreement between 'opponents' who have hitherto held different opinions. That person alone is a lover of peace who is even prepared to accept defeat in a division of opinion, who is prepared in principle to admit his 'opponent' to be in the right, who is willing to end the discussion with a different attitude from that with which he started it. That person alone is a lover of peace who can bring himself to commend the very person whose opinions and decisions he thought he had to oppose and resist. That person alone is a lover of peace who shows politeness and patience even to someone who gets on his nerves.

We are peace-loving only if we classify the attitudes and endeavours of others as little as possible under simple, general concepts which can easily be rejected, if we are constantly overcoming also our thinking in clichés, constantly making the effort to see behind the words the reality itself, on which perhaps there is no real disagreement. We are peace-loving only if we measure *ourselves* by the ideal but *others* by what is really possible, if we don't defend our social prestige, if we fight honestly and fairly even though this fairness diminishes our chances of victory. We serve peace only if we really understand that it is possible to incur responsibility even by hesitation and silence, if we respect politicians only when they prove themselves otherwise to be men and not merely the representatives of our own selfishness, if we distrust politicians particularly when they are much too ready to admit that we are in the right and to confirm our own opinions.

The gospel blessing on peacemakers comes upon us only if we defend not only our own but also others' freedom, if we slowly learn to be really sensitive not only to the wrong done to ourselves but likewise to wrong done to others. The peace-lover also possesses little, ordinary virtues: he is polite to those over whom he himself has power and does not cringe before those who are more powerful than he is; he draws the attention of a person in the wrong to his mistakes and keeps silent about them before others; he does not insist on his own importance and does not consider himself irreplaceable; he knows that for all of us self-criticism burns itself out more quickly than self-defence, that we should be able to give up responsibility and should not think that we ourselves can do all for the best; he knows that it may occasionally be better for the other to do something *well* than for ourselves to have done it *better*, since the other's freedom – which is the really better – can flourish only when he is allowed to do well what he can do.

The peace-lover does not allow any brutal alternatives to be forced upon him; he tries to formulate the arguments of his opponent better and more convincingly than the latter can do himself, since the peace-lover does not want to gain a cheap victory by making a fool of his opponent. The peace-lover will not be one-sided when he sees that this is the result of jumping to conclusions, because he knows that we are still one-sided when we think that we can see all sides.

The peace-lover is polite when politeness is likely to be to his own detriment and perhaps considers bluntness appropriate when politeness could only be to his advantage. The peace-lover respects the 'signs of the times', but he does not worship them. He does not think that God is always on the side of the big battalions. He plays his part, calmly and boldly, knowing that others have a different part and that the symphony of the world sounds quite convincing, not where we, the individual players, stand and play, but where the sound is heard of one only, of God.

Creative hope and peace

Someone who wants to fulfil his mandate for peace must be hopeful and begin his action for peace at the point where he is at the time. The peace which is not yet, but for which we have a mandate, that peace, that is, which is still to come, can come to be only as a result of historical acts freely undertaken. This peace is not only the spontaneously emerging product of a necessary evolution in the economic, social, and political dimensions. This peace is really future, it has to be achieved; it is not simply there already, concealed in the present. But future can be made only by those who hope. Future is first of all always Utopia, which only the hopeful person can plan and seize for himself in advance. Future is that which is recklessly willed in complete freedom, without reinsurance, and in this sense it is what is hoped for as distinct from what is merely planned and calculated.

Without this creative hope the peace of the future cannot come: without the hope which is action and not mere cosy expectation.

This future peace cannot be achieved by creative hope as an

isolated, individual work which might be completed within the sphere of our own existence without affecting or changing other things within that sphere. The peace of the future is rather the result of much more far-reaching and radical changes which transform our whole existence. To say that peace is the work of justice is to see it as derived from the whole of human existence. Only when a higher justice permeates all dimensions of existence, when far-reaching changes of awareness and very substantial changes in all social institutionalisms are successful, can the peace of the future come.

The mandate of creative hope for peace is therefore by its very nature extended to the creative action of hope for a very radical change of man, his society, and his environment. Hope for peace becomes hope for the one future in its wholeness which is entrusted to man as his deed. This whole future is certainly in the first place an intramundane future. But this latter is in fact also the necessary mediation of that eschatological hope which means God himself and gains from this standpoint its final worth and the radical seriousness with which it lays claim to us as its hopeful agents.

Peace of a new future

Peace is only another name for the whole future successfully achieved; but at present that future is shrouded in darkness. It cannot be calculated merely in the planning offices of the futurologists, since these in the last resort can know the future only as implied in the present, not the really new future of creative hope, however much that which can be calculated and planned may enter into this new future and the planning itself be a factor of the creative hope. If the mandate of peace is extended and elevated in this way to the greater mandate of the new future and to a creative hope, it must not be understood as ideologically innocuous, as if hoping were mere expectation and the new future as a whole only that which makes demands on *nobody* precisely because it is the mission of *all*. Although it is an act of freedom, creative Utopia of the new future in hope is certainly also the incalculable gift of history and its Lord. So too is the peace of this new future.

We should, however, be liars if we were to say that we are the ones who hope for this future and its peace, unless at the point where we stand here and now we are doing what serves the cause of peace. But we are doing this only if each of us in his own place, in his own particular situation, in regard to the people he is constantly meeting, succeeds in thought, word, and deed in overcoming his selfishness. This does not mean restricting our peace-mandate merely to ethics and to a field that is prior to the social and political sphere, for this very act of gaining a real victory over our selfishness simply cannot take place merely within the field of interpersonal relationships. This act itself has always a social dimension, social consequences which, however slowly, change the institutionalisms of society.

Opinions may well be and remain very divided on how radical such changes will have to be in order to produce the peace of the new future, whether they can be effected in many small steps or only by great revolutionary moves; but the recognition of this fact and the obligation of tolerance involved in it must not be made an excuse for those who really want no change and therefore no true peace. But in any case, in such a situation, someone who is thinking more in evolutionary terms, who advocates many small steps towards a true peace, must ask himself whether this is what he is really doing or whether his programme merely conceals the fact that he wants to stay where he is. And anyone who thinks that only large steps, only radical changes in society, can serve true peace in a new future, anyone who fights for this view, must likewise see that he is bound nevertheless to gain small victories over his own egoism until greater moves and revolutionary changes are actually possible. For, without such modest victories over the egoism concealed almost to the point of identity in all of us, even the most far-reaching social revolutions would mean no more than the replacement of one tyranny by another, a new form of war and not true peace. The small steps are for all part of the mandate of peace, for, if they are really taken, there is already concealed in them secretly and almost invisibly the miracle of creative hope, the quiet dawn of a new future.

ORDINARY VIRTUES

'Ordinary vitrues' is an odd expression. Everyone thinks that the meaning of 'ordinariness' is clear, although this is not really so: it means just what is constantly happening, with its routine, its biological and social constraints, the flatness of feelings and experiences, the same duties and necessities constantly recurring, having to do with the same people and in the end ceasing to notice them. 'Virtue' is a word which has become suspect today. We don't like 'paragons of virtue' very much; we suspect that striving to be virtuous is a sign of introversion, of moral arrogance, which does not befit someone who thinks dispassionately of life's real task and of his fellow-men. Hence 'ordinary virtues' sounds suspicious.

And yet this term too is obvious enough. For where, except in ordinary life, are we to practise punctuality, consideration for others, reliability, a certain equanimity, the effort not to make others suffer from our moodiness and bad temper, tolerance, readiness to discuss differences of opinion quietly and objectively with one another, a humour which prevents us from taking ourselves too seriously, good manners and politeness, and so many other virtues? Without them ordinary life itself would become unbearable.

Whether they should all be called 'virtues' is in the last resort a matter of indifference. But no one can seriously maintain that all that belongs in this way to a bearable, ordinary human life exists simply and solely as a result of 'breeding', of childhood training. These things must constantly be acquired in self-criticism, in a serious effort, and in self-control: to put it in an old-fashioned way, we must 'practise virtue'.

Evidently, then, there are such things as ordinary virtues, even though the motives for practising and seeking to acquire them may be very varied, and even though it is *a priori* obvious that, first of all at any rate, we do not have to bring the most sublime ethical motives to the realization of these ordinary virtues; but their nature is precisely such that a reasonable and decent person takes them for granted and therefore doesn't look for any profound ethical and religious foundation for them. In fact they function better, the less we make a problem of them, the more they belong to those psychical habits induced by discipline and mechanisms which work spontaneously and thus free the moral subject precisely for his great decisions, since the ordinary virtues do not themselves use up much of what we may call 'moral energy'.

However, in apparent contradiction to what has just been said, we may be permitted to reflect a little on these ordinary virtues. Anyway, people reflect on many things which are still more unobtrusive and insignificant and mostly function best when their course is not interrupted by too much reflection.

Ordinariness of grace

Ordinary virtues mean for the Christian the ordinariness of grace. What grace, its realization in faith, hope, and love, its growth and ripening, mean in Christian terms cannot of course be explained at length here. Nevertheless, it must be pointed out that man's existence and his personal history of freedom have an infinite depth, are open to the mystery of God and of his self-communication which we call grace. The event of this grace in human life occurs, however, not merely in sublime, isolated moments and thus not only in the ultimate decisions of our life, not only in explicit prayer, in receiving the sacraments, in explicitly religious basic experiences.

The difference between ordinary life and the sublime and sacred hours of destiny in a human life should certainly not be smoothed out. We shall have to speak of this later. But first of all it is important to say clearly that man's whole life in personal knowledge and freedom, and thus too in its ordinariness, is the history of grace. However little the Christian can forego moments in his life of explicit prayer, of liturgical worship of God, of express praise and thanksgiving to God in the holy community of the Church, hours of questioning and answering when he decides before God on the direction which his life is to take, it is equally impossible to restrict to a particular area of his life his religious life, his faith, his relationship to God, or whatever we like to call it. His life is worldly and secular, involves 'intramundane' tasks and goals, is interpersonal communication; but it is in these very things – provided only that a basic decision for God exists, sustained by God's grace – that the life of grace occurs, his religious existence is realized, his eternal life comes to be. All this in the midst of ordinary life, through it and not merely passing it by.

If a Christian were to think that his relationship to God is realized only in the expressly and thematically religious or even merely ecclesial field, he would need to have his mentality and his life 'desacralized'. The directly religious and sacral occurrences of his life – which are certainly necessary – only render explicit the association with God which, however silently and wordlessly, goes on in the whole length and breadth of his life, that is, in the very midst of his ordinary life. In textbook language we might say that, where a person freely following the dictate of his conscience sees, accepts, and realizes a moral value, a human demand, arising out of the concreteness of his life, there always exists also in the concrete order of salvation the event of grace, its growing and ripening, even if this ultimate depth of his life does not exist as conceptually objectified at the particular moment.

This holds therefore for ordinary life and its virtues. In them the religious is secularized and at the same time the secular is sanctified, an event of eternal life in man. Textbook theology tries to make this more intelligible in the light of considerations into which we shall not enter more closely here. It speaks of a 'virtual intention' in regard to God and eternal life which can exist prior to reflection in the believer and justified person, and which sustains the individual actions of his life, even if he does not reflect on this. It speaks of man's individual actions being permeated and shaped by the 'infused', habitual, supernatural, theological virtues of faith, hope, and charity. All these and many other formulas of textbook theology, which we shall pass over here, are meant really to express only this one thing: that the religious element, the element of grace, in human life does not constitute a special zone in man's life outside of which there is only the purely profane and secular, without meaning for man's existence as oriented to God, but – presupposing an ultimate decision of faith, in love for God, which again itself can be very unthematic and exist even in atheists – that personal and practical life in personal knowledge and freedom is identical with the life of grace. And this holds, as we have said, necessarily also for man's ordinary life in so far as his ordinary life is a real factor in this personal existence.

From the theological standpoint all this is obvious. But nothing can be taken for granted in the life of the average Christian. He always thinks that religious life, the history of his personal association with God, begins and is realized only when he explicitly prays or receives the sacraments as 'means of grace'. Hence he appreciates then the interpersonal significance and the practical utility of the ordinary virtues, but does not know of their ultimate depth in which they too are mysteriously filled with God himself, with the incomprehensible mystery of his life.

Littleness of ordinary life

We must consider the ordinary virtues now from quite another aspect, without, however, taking back what has just been said. Ordinary life is and remains ordinary life. This is obvious from our constant experience that we human beings, subject to space and time, cannot force the whole depth and the whole radical character of our life's free decision into each individual moment of our existence. This can be taken for granted. In biblical terms, we are not always involved with our whole heart, our whole mind, and all our strength, in everything we do, whether as tending to God, in our relations with our fellow-men, or in face of our proper life-task. Although a unity in its origin, in the personal subject, and as directed to our life's finality before God, our existence is in a sense 'dispersed' over the breadth of a temporal life.

Until we die, our existence is only rarely or perhaps never radically 'concentrated' into one single moment. This in fact is just what constitutes our ordinary life and is also the ultimate reason why we simply cannot draw an exact dividing line between the ordinary 'distractedness' of our existence and the really ultimate basic decisions into which we concentrate our whole existence. The apparently very great, rare hours of our life (an adult baptism, a choice of vocation, a wedding, Holy Communion, etc.), seen existentially, may be very ordinary : that is, we are not really wholly involved with the last resources of our freedom in a personal commitment; and, on the other hand, the ultimate decisions of our life take place in an apparently ordinary occurrence on which we have reflected very little.

What does all this mean in more exact theological terms in regard to the 'nature' of ordinary life? In order to see more clearly at this point, we shall start out from some theological data which are dogmatically certain and also obvious to the Christian possessed of a normal catechism knowledge, even though this starting point may seem rather odd within the framework of our reflections. We are referring to the distinction between 'grave' and 'venial' sins. We must, however, assume a number of things which cannot be more closely substantiated or explained here: the very existence of this far from obvious distinction; its significance for religion and not merely for theology; its objective reality, even though the line of demarcation between these two kinds of sin cannot be drawn with absolute certainty in concrete life; objectively and subjectively, it is not merely a distinction between 'more' and 'less', but a very radical distinction between two essentially different human activities which can only very analogously be subsumed under the one word 'sin'. The important thing here is the fact – obvious enough in itself, but simply not mentioned or mentioned only marginally in the normal moral theology – that this essential distinction between human free decisions must evidently hold also for free decisions which are morally *good*.

There is not even a word in current use in religious and theological language for this distinction in the field of positive moral behaviour. We must perhaps first invent one, but our terminology is bound to be clumsy and merely provisional. For want of a better terminology and in the hope nevertheless of being understood, we may say that, if there are grave and slight sins and if there is a radical distinction between them, there are also necessarily voluntary *good* 'grave' and 'slight' human acts and between them there exists the same very radical distinction as that which exists between grave and venial sins. This means that there are decisions in which a person places his whole existence so freely in face of an objectively significant reality of his life that this decision radically determines his relationship to God for life or death; and there are human acts which are 'free' and have a certain moral significance, but do not dispose of one's own existence as a whole in this way before God. There are then, as Aquinas would say, decisions about the goal and decisions merely about particular ways and means to this goal.

Since this distinction arises from the spatial-temporal, flesh and blood, 'concupiscent' nature of man, who can become aware of himself only through the mediation of a particular reality other than himself, it must exist, as we have said, both between morally good and morally bad actions. All this we have said briefly and by way of suggestions. But, if it is accepted, we can define with some measure of theological accuracy the essence of ordinary life and ordinary virtues: ordinary life is good and ordinary virtues exist whenever there is a question of morally 'slight' and not of 'grave' acts in the sense described.

In this way, however, the acts of the ordinary virtues seem to decline in significance: they seem indeed to retain their usefulness for ordinary life and for the common life of men, but it is no longer easy to see that they are properly a part of that realization of grace of which we spoke at first.

Dialectic of the littleness of ordinary life and the basic decision of freedom

If we are to maintain the significance of the acts of ordinary life as events of the life of grace, in the light of the theological explanation just given, we might first of all appeal to the common Christian understanding and appraisal of 'virtuous' ordinary life in which, it is generally understood, the infused theological and moral virtues are brought into action.

In order, however, to see better that such an appraisal of ordinary life does not rest merely on pious optimism, the relationship between 'grave' and 'slight' good acts (to continue using our adopted terminology) must be more closely defined. We must not imagine human life in personal freedom and free self-disposal as a mere series of acts succeeding one another in time, each existing in itself and all of them being capable of being summed up only in a moral calculation which is external to them. Despite its temporal extension and the plurality of acts which, compared with each other, have not the same existential significance, the personal mental and free life of a human being is a real unity in which all the elements, even though temporally plural, are mutually interdependent. Every act which is done 'now', even though of varying intensity and importance, is the expression and result of the whole of a person's previous life: the past remains present in this one life and is not merely 'added in' by a moral judge (God, for example).

In this one personal life, therefore, there are certainly basic attitudes which are constantly manifested in the apparently very casual series of individual actions, in a sense always freshly 'ratified' by new voluntary acts. Such basic attitudes, as long as they are not merely 'gifts' of nature or grace but really belong to the moral subject, as such responsible for himself, are set up and accepted through basic decisions of human freedom: that is, precisely through what we hitherto described from another starting point as 'grave' human acts. These basic decisions, which freely set up such basic attitudes, can of course be made very explicitly and 'thematically': in a radical religious conversion, on the occasion of other decisions of a lifetime made after mature reflection. But it must not necessarily always be so.

Basic decisions and basic attitudes (in the sense described) cannot indeed be established and in principle are not conceivable without the realization of that radical freedom in which the subject itself as a whole is really involved. But we cannot on that account simply say that there can be such a basic decision only if it is given objective expression as such by the free subject in an explicitly conceptual moral theme. To take an extreme example, it is quite possible for someone to consider himself an atheist in his conceptual reflection and nevertheless to be a theist in the unthematic but radically authentic exercise of his moral responsibility. For our subsequent reflection – thus, for example, for our 'examination of conscience' – it is therefore never possible to say with *absolute* certainty where, when, and how such ultimate basic decisions have taken place. If we knew this, we would have to know also with absolute certainty in our reflection on ourselves whether we are in 'a state of grace'; but, according to the teaching of the Council of Trent, this is denied us.

We may well regard as such a personal basic decision some event which is really only the comparatively innocuous, even though – seen from outside – very important, consequence of a basic decision which took place at quite a different point in our lives, much more unobtrusively and casually but nevertheless in radical freedom. And an event of our life, insignificant if regarded from outside and biographically, may certainly have involved real and radical decisions which stamp our subsequent life for ever or for a long time and up to a point form the law and the table of values set up in freedom, according to which our subsequent life is shaped.

From this standpoint a deeper understanding can be acquired of the relationship between the 'grave' acts and the 'slight' actions which constitute our ordinary life. Ultimate, basic decisions can be expressed and manifested in 'slight' acts of ordinary life; they can be better presented and more easily tested critically in insignificant occurrences of ordinary life than in themselves, at the moment when they take place, without reflection and unthematically, without being given an explicit moral label. On the other hand, such 'slight' acts of ordinary life can even be the unremarkable and casual event in which such basic decisions themselves occur, in which ultimate basic attitudes are adopted. Hence it becomes obvious that we can define, as we did above, *in the abstract*, in theological terms, ordinary actions as 'slight'; but, in the always subsequent reflection, never adequately objectifying the whole realization of freedom, we can never say for certain whether any particular event in the course of our life was such a 'slight' action of ordinary life or a 'grave' decision marking a great and rare hour in the movement of our history of freedom towards its end. Ordinary life can be distinguished theoretically from the hours of destiny in the history of our eternity, and the distinction exists in real life, but where and how this distinction occurs in the concrete we can never determine in our reflection. What seems like a great hour may perhaps be only a moment of ordinary life, and what we call ordinary life may be filled, secretly and unobtrusively, with decisive moments of eternity.

Moral theology is entirely right in theory in requiring for a 'grave' (good or bad) act a correspondingly important object, *materia gravis*: so, for example, some inattentiveness at prayer, even if it is 'voluntary', cannot be objectively a grave sin. The same of course could be said of good acts, if they are to be 'grave'. But this proposition, correct in itself, holds only if we are considering a single act in isolation and simply on its own account (which, of course, is methodologically possible). Integrated into the greater whole of a life or section of life, such a 'slight matter' of a voluntary action can have a quite different character, can be the object of a 'grave' moral decision, the material on which this decision can certainly be exercised. How easy it is, for example, to think of the really culpable breakdown of a marriage as the result of an action, a word, a gesture, inattention: in a word, of things which seem to be no more than the innocuous trivialities of ordinary life.

Briefly summing up, we can say that ordinary virtuous actions may be the manifestation and expression of ultimate, basic decisions made in grace, shaping an eternity; they may indeed be trivial events in which and behind which such a basic decision freshly made is concealed. For both reasons, such acts of the ordinary virtues, in spite of the fundamental and necessary distinction between slight and grave, can be realizations of the life of grace itself.

Waiting for the coming of the Lord

If we are to perceive the moral and religious significance of these ordinary virtues, a further peculiarity in the plural unity of the history of human freedom must be noticed. Particularly for its great and radical basic decisions, freedom needs a situation which makes them possible, since the creature's freedom is a responsive freedom which must first be given a word that can be answered. Even to the free subject as such not everything is possible at every moment. Hence ordinary life in itself, if we do not ideologize or heroize it in a pseudo-asceticism, is the very time when what is great and decisive in life is not possible, when the situation provides scope only for 'slight' voluntary acts. In biblical terms, the *kairos* of a life's decision assigned by God does not exist at all times, since it is a grace bestowed by God here and not there, however much Scripture also regards the one whole of human life and the situation given with Christ as an always pressing, once and for all given *kairos* for the decision for or against God. But just because this *kairos* of the decision of our one and entire life's history is not at our autonomous disposal, because we must answer when we are asked, we must be waiting and ready: in biblical terms again, we must be waiting and watching as servants, not knowing the hour of the Lord's coming.

We cannot identify this hour simply with the cosmic second coming of Christ or with the unforeseeable hour of our death. God breaks into our life with his grace, his judgement, and his salvation, radically and unexpectedly wherever and whenever a decision is made which (allowing for all the intrinsic possibilities of conversion and defection) becomes the permanent law of our life. But we must be watching and ready for such hours of God's coming. In the last resort the unexpected must not surprise us, even though God will not blame man living in time for needing a certain time really to cope with such decisive situations in life. This waiting and this being ready, *all* this, is certainly not an additional occupation which we have to carry on alongside our ordinary life. A part of this ordinary life is certainly an 'ordinary' expressly religious life. But, allowing for this, ordinary life with its ordinary virtues is itself this waiting in readiness for the great hours in which we decide our eternal lot. In the light of this fact the ordinary virtues once again have their own seriousness and their fateful significance.

We cannot, of course, assert that someone who is well-behaved and devout, virtuous in his ordinary life, is also already certain that he will survive the great situations where it is a question of life or death. The grace of such endurance is a grace which no one can merit by his good behaviour in ordinary life. But ordinary life is indeed the way in which we must remain ready for the decisive situations; it can be the way in which God wants to give us the very grace – which we cannot demand – of surviving the great hours of our life, even though it may constantly happen through God's free disposition that someone who has only moderately or badly mastered his ordinary life may still endure his great hour. This grace too exists. But we may not presume on it, we must be faithful in little things in order to be permitted to hope that God in his grace will also send us faithfulness in great things. In the light of this, too, the small ordinary virtues are something great.

Liberation for the objective task and for the obvious

We can attempt to see the nature of the ordinary virtues from another aspect. Freedom in its metaphysical and theological sense is freedom of the subject to dispose of itself, not simply that freedom of choice which is exercised only about impersonal things. And since morality properly so-called together with its religious dimension exists only where there is freedom, the moral is characterized by the reference of the subject to itself, it is essentially 'subjective'. On the other hand, the moral exists only where someone 'does something for its own sake', where man gets away from himself, succeeds in overcoming an introverted subjectivity, and finds 'a taste for reality as it is in itself' (*sapere res prout sunt*), as is evident even from *The Imitation of Christ* in spite of its late-medieval pious introvertedness. The moral thus lies necessarily in the field of tension of these two poles, it is necessarily the 'most subjective' and the 'most objective' at the same time, inward turning and outward turning in one. This is seen most clearly in love which embraces all that is moral, which is the 'bond of perfection'. Love is the total involvement of the subject and must love the other precisely for his own sake and not for the sake of experiencing the subjective happiness of love.

Perhaps it may also be said that this polarity which exists in all that is moral is itself constantly being modified afresh and has a history in the life of the individual and of mankind. The polarity does not always exist in the same way in every moral act. Firstly the subject is itself confronted and saddled with its solitary subjectivity and inalienable responsibility, so that the always necessary mediation of the categorial reality on which all freedom must be exercised seems almost to have disappeared. Secondly, the subject itself almost disappears in the dispassionate surrender to the objective task which is committed to it in virtue of its spatial-temporal and social situation. This hither and thither between the two poles is a factor in the individual subject's history of freedom and varies greatly with different individuals in its specific character. This polarity is associated, even though not simply identical, with the indissoluble unity and diversity which exist in the moral sphere between disposition and achievement.

Considering all this, we may perhaps say rather cautiously that the deeds of the ordinary virtues are characterized by that form of the polarity mentioned in which the subject gets away from himself to the matter in hand, from the disposition to the achievement, in which the objective predominates over the subjective within this permanent polarity.

In the light of this the ordinary virtues once again acquire a very special importance. Where the subject is quite closely and almost immediately aware of itself in its moral decision, there arises also the mortal danger to morals that the subject may begin to enjoy its own subjectivity as moral and thus in the end destroy it. The lover no longer loves the other person, but only his own love; the morally faithful person no longer really applies himself in self-forgetfulness to his task, so that the latter may gain its rightness and its reality, but is proud of his fidelity, enjoys his independence; being moral is taken to be its own reward. It is here that the deeds of the ordinary virtues have their great importance. They are really never such as to be their own reward. They appear always as something that can be taken for granted, about which no one makes a fuss. For this very reason they can be an exercise in real moral behaviour, in self-forgetfulness: ultimately, therefore, the practice of that love which goes out to the other person and no longer reflects narcissistically on itself.

Anonymity of ordinary life

Up to now we have spoken about the ordinary virtues in a very abstract and general way: in other words, we have been doing something which is always contrary to their real nature. We ought to speak of the concrete ordinary virtues in such a way that the very word 'virtue' practically never occurs; we ought at the same time to avoid moralizing, in order to state the sober facts of ordinary life, which has to be lived realistically and without a lot of talk. But understandably this is not possible here, since ordinary life itself, in its modern highly complex nature, would have to be described: how it emerges today out of all that constitutes the individual and social life of man. We should have to draw up a list of ordinary virtues, which presumably is impossible.

Virtues and vices have indeed been catalogued from the earliest times of philosophical ethics through the New Testament up to the moral theology and moral philosophy of the present time. In these lists, based on systems which in the last resort remain very arbitrary and questionable, virtues are certainly designated which might be considered as specifically ordinary virtues. Think, for example, of *eutrapelia* which found its way from Aristotelian ethics into the systematic moral theology of Aquinas. But, as far as I know, there is no systematic treatment of the ordinary virtues as such.

This is not a misfortune. Not only because these ordinary virtues in the last resort are only the concrete form of the higher virtues in ordinary life, but also because the continual changes in ordinary life must constantly give rise to new ordinary virtues. Where, for example, there is no motorized traffic, we cannot seriously speak of a traffic morality of ordinary life. There remain, therefore, many virtues without a moral-theological label. On the one hand, this is good, since we should act morally in ordinary life but without moral pomposity. But it is also unfortunate, because people are not made sufficiently aware of much that ought to be done in ordinary life.

We may, however, console ourselves for the anonymity of the ordinary virtues with a final reflection. The distinction between morality and morals is well known. These two factors are not identical, but are closely related to each other. Morals (the 'ethos' of a particular time, of a social group, etc.) are the concrete expression of morality, related to the historically conditioned situation of a period or of a social group; they sum up the rules of the game and regulate the life of a particular time or group; they provide the concrete expression of the ultimate binding morality, even though always in an historically and sociologically conditioned and therefore changeable form. We might thus say that the morals of a time and of a group are the sum-total of the ordinary virtues which common life in a particular time or group requires of the individual. The spontaneity and anonymity of many ordinary virtues are certainly characteristic also of the way in which the morals of an age or of a group are simply taken for granted without further analysis.

5
Living Testimony

TERESA OF AVILA
DOCTOR OF THE CHURCH

Teresa has been declared a Doctor of the Church. This event naturally has some significance for the position and function of woman in the Church. The charism of teaching – and indeed of teaching directed to the Church as such – is not merely a male prerogative. The idea of woman being less gifted in an intellectual or religious sense is thus repudiated. It is thus expressly recognized that women may study theology, particularly since charism and the study of theology methodically accomplished cannot be regarded as opposites.

It should not be said that Teresa is an exception. For all Doctors of the Church, the men too among them, are exceptions. And the proclamation declaring her a Doctor of the Church makes it clear that women have not previously been given this title not because none of them was worthy of it, but because of reasons rooted in the cultural status of woman at the time. This proclamation clearly shows that I Corinthians 14.34 is a time-conditioned norm (justified at the time) imposed by the Apostle Paul.

People may of course wonder whether naming Teresa a Doctor of the Church is merely a handsome gesture, meant in the last resort to provide an excuse for not entrusting to women living in the Church today those tasks or recognizing those rights which are due to them and which they are still far from possessing fully and as something that is really obvious. We may wonder also whether women themselves in the Church today are really prepared to accept the position and function which they can have if they want them.

Teacher of mysticism

Teresa is proclaimed as a teacher of mysticism. This means first of all that a person who teaches something about mysticism is doing theology, is speaking in the light of revelation, saying something to the Church as such for the edification of the faithful. This is itself of supreme importance. For it is by no means so obvious at first sight that the 'mysticism' which Teresa and John of the Cross put forward has to do with revelation and theological teaching in the Church as such. The fact that Christ or grace is mentioned in this teaching on mysticism is not itself a proof that this unique relatedness of consciousness to the things of which faith speaks – which is described by both as mystical – really belongs as such to the sphere of revealed theology.

Why is mystical experience not the opposite of faith? How far is mysticism in Teresa's sense more than a natural transformation of consciousness (produced perhaps parapsychologically or psycho-technically), which as such has nothing to do with the workings of grace or at most – like other 'natural' factors of consciousness – merely provides the natural basis which grace, according to the theologians, always presupposes? Is mysticism simply a stage (albeit a high one) on the way of Christian life, or is it an almost miraculous phenomenon which God alone produces outside the normal course of Christian life? If the first alternative is correct, does this 'normality' consist in the fact that mysticism in the Christian sense is the Christian achievement in the light of faith and under the influence of grace of a stage in a natural psycho-logical development accessible in principle to every human being? Or is it simply the 'normality' of a specifically supernatural develop-ment of the life of grace as such?

These and similar questions arise with fresh urgency if we take seriously the declaration that Teresa is a Doctor of the Church and do not try to see in it merely a timely gesture in regard to woman in the Church today. Such questions are still far from being answered sufficiently clearly and unanimously. The reason is not that a modern history of religion, a history of piety and a modern psychology of religion, at a time when the Church is turning in a wholly new way and more impartially than formerly to the non-Christian religions, can discover much more 'mysticism' outside the Church than the Christian theologians could do in the past. But the question then arises as to whether mysticism outside Christianity (which certainly exists) is an 'anonymously' Christian and therefore grace-inspired mysticism. Or, on the other hand, is Christian mysticism a 'natural' mysticism just like non-Christian, although obviously under the influence of grace like all other free, moral actions of a human being, purified and free from baser elements like all that is naturally moral? Or are these two questions aimed after all at the same thing?

Mysticism within the present horizon of understanding

The declaration of St Teresa as Doctor of the Church comes at a time when a 'Death of God' theology is being developed, in which God is said to count only as a mythological cipher for the radicalness of interpersonal human relations, in which we have the impression that God can no longer be discovered in a radically secularized, self-sufficient world. But even today it is still possible, indeed it is more urgent than ever, to have a theology and, even beyond this, an initiation into man's personal experience of God. And the classical authorities on Spanish mysticism are thoroughly good and almost irreplaceable teachers of this sort of theology and initiation, particularly adept at making this personal experience of God intelligible.

If these older mystics are to be able to help us in this task, we must of course assume for our part that in every human being (as a result of the nature of the mind and of the grace of the divine self-communication always offered to everyone) there is something like an anonymous, unthematic, perhaps repressed, basic experience of being oriented to God, which is constitutive of man in his concrete make-up (of nature and grace), which can be repressed but not destroyed, which is 'mystical' or (if you prefer a more cautious terminology) has its climax in what the older teachers called infused contemplation.

Of course we ought to read these classical writers with other eyes than those of a devout contemplative of former times, for whom the temptation from atheism scarcely existed. Of course we ought to translate the psychology of these masters with their terminology, their perspectives, their assumptions of what they regarded as obvious, and so on, into a modern existential ontology and modern theological anthropology. For, however 'descriptive' the mystical theology of these classical writers may be as compared with that of their predecessors, it still is not and cannot be a pure description, since the very experience they are describing is itself shaped up to a point by a time-conditioned element of interpretation. But the carrying over of this description of mystical experience into modern horizons of understanding is possible in principle, even though it has scarcely been attempted, since teachers of mystical theology even up to recent decades simply continued to speak the language of the classical masters. And such a translation could be fruitful, since the depth and radicality of the experience of God which these classical writers describe are not so familiar that we could discover in ourselves its starting points and traces just as easily without their help as with it.

With reference to these themes, the question may then perhaps arise as to whether the work of the great Teresa or that of John of the Cross could be more helpful to a modern theology and initiation into the experience of God. We might at first perhaps think that the radical 'absence of images' in the experience of God as described by John of the Cross would make him a better interpreter of our modern experience of God than Teresa with her more frankly visionary mysticism. But if we consider that the loss of imagery today is to be counted precisely *as* a loss and not as a gain, if we see that our relationship to God today must either be mediated perhaps more explicitly than ever through our relationship to the concrete Jesus of Nazareth, to his life and death and his relationship to his fellow-men, or it will not exist at all, then it is perhaps not so obvious that for us today Teresa of Avila must rank behind John of the Cross. The fact that her desire for penance did not lessen her appreciation of good roast partridge and that she was also an incomparably worldly-wise organizer and diplomat (which John of the Cross certainly was not): these are also things which make her mysticism particularly sympathetic to us today.

THINKER AND CHRISTIAN
OBITUARY OF ROMANO GUARDINI

Yesterday evening [1 October 1968] a great man, a thinker, and a Christian entered into that peace in which he had always believed, which he had always sought. In a brief first obituary it is of course impossible to appraise the man and his work in a way that does justice to Romano Guardini. But even now it is right to say something about the importance of this great Christian in the fields of religion, theology, and the history of ideas.

First of all, a couple of biographical notes. Romano Guardini was born in Verona and was therefore Italian by birth. But he spent all his youth in Germany, in Mainz, without on that account ever denying his Latin and classical origins. He became a priest in the diocese of Mainz. From 1923 to 1939 he was professor of philosophy of religion and Catholic *Weltanschauung* in Berlin until deprived of his professorship by the National Socialists. From 1945 to 1947 he again held the same chair at the university of Tübingen, and from then onwards up to an advanced age at the university of Munich. He was honoured by the Church with the title of Monsignor and by the German authorities with the order *pour le mérite* for arts and science.

Even to provide only a rough appraisal of Guardini's literary, theological, and philological work and of his contributions to the history of ideas, we should have to outline the contents of more than a hundred books. This is completely impossible. We cannot here estimate the value of the work of the religious awakener, the interpreter of Scripture, the pioneer of the liturgical movement, the preacher, the prophetical critic of our age, the interpreter of great figures in the history of ideas from antiquity until the present time, the phenomenologist of basic human attitudes, the theologian. We shall therefore consider merely the place of Guardini's work in our most recent past and in the present, what it means and what effects it produces there.

Even this question is not easy to answer properly. For it depends firstly on the general interpretation to be given of this recent past and present, and, secondly, it still does not touch the really unique character of his work, which was meant to serve only the eternal in man, his original and authentic relationship to God, as it is lived and not merely talked about. All this in countless pages telling of man and thus seeking to tell of God who is the true mystery of man.

If nevertheless we are to attempt to the best of our ability an answer free from subjective and arbitrary interpretation and therefore with no claim to any particular originality, perhaps it would be well to point to three simple facts. Guardini became a priest at that period of Church history when the fear of 'modernism' and the reaction to it dominated intellectual life in the Church; his life's work began after the First World War and the evening of his life came at the time of the Council.

What happened during this period? While maintaining her dogmatic and thus ultimately decisive self-understanding, the Church has ceased to regard herself as an intellectually, culturally and humanly self-sufficient, closed society, on the defensive, seeking to win support by her conservatism; now, without prejudice, although at peril to herself, she plunges into the situation of the time, giving and also ready to receive, sharing the problems and the perils of the time, bursting into a new age which even she cannot plan in advance, serving and concerned not with herself but with men.

The Church's fight against modernism was certainly a resolute and victorious struggle to maintain her ultimate theological self-understanding, her possession of a divine revelation and an authorization coming from God and not from men. But, from the empirical standpoint, it was also the struggle of an integralism seeking to impose an ecclesiastical administration on the whole of life; a neo-scholasticism refusing to take up a positive attitude to modern philosophy, with a thought- and life-style belonging to the 'Restoration' of the first half of the nineteenth century, not in accordance either with the great tradition of the Church or with its own time, not able to keep alive the legitimate heritage of the *philosophia perennis*; a social and hierarchical conservatism which assumed that God's truth and grace could not be found everywhere, but only in the ivory tower which the Church had built for herself from the time of the Enlightenment onwards.

The Church lost this battle against modernism, because by her very nature she could not keep it up in the long run. Externally and historically this struggle was broken off by the mental caesura created by the First World War. But the fact that this reactionary-conservative period came to an end internally is really due to the contribution – which could not have been taken for granted at the time – made by a comparatively few men in Western and Central Europe whom I cannot list here. But Romano Guardini is certainly one of them and not the least important. The hard times of modernism and integralism certainly left deep scars on these men. And it certainly could not be assumed after the First World War that the old struggle would not break out again. The fact that it did not happen is God's grace which he bestowed on the Church in these men: for they found the word – which was seen only later to be obvious – which could be understood by the institutional Church and their own time.

In the important reference work, *Religion in Geschichte und Gegenwart*, Guardini is made a representative of *Kulturkatholizismus*. This sort of label is superficial and even silly. But there is some truth in it. The men of whom I am speaking, and Guardini in particular, suddenly succeeded in showing in an exemplary fashion in word and deed that it was possible to be openly a man of our time and of modern civilization and at the same time a Catholic Christian; that it was possible to be a man of the modern age and thus too to be able and to have to dissociate oneself critically from his own time with his rationality, his subjectivity, his personality, his experience of autonomy and freedom, to be free from resentment towards one's own time and its attitudes and yet without either succumbing to it uncritically or abandoning attempts to be truly 'modern'; that it was possible also to have the courage to be unmodern and instead to stand by God's truth and the greater wealth of an unrejected tradition.

These men taught the German Church, and thus slowly the Church as a whole, to live in a pluralistic world without becoming relativistic, so to relate the gospel message that it is not completely unintelligible even to outsiders, to give the one Christian reality a form that can be seen as broadly common to the Christian denominations, to make present-day language express the meaning of sacred architecture and art, to discern what is Christian even where it is opposed to our own traditional thought- and life-style. If the crisis of modernism, in spite of all individual distress and personal tragedy, was overcome comparatively quickly; if the

Church's development in philosophy, theology, liturgy, in her life and in her association with the intellectual-cultural life of the period from after the First World War until now, in spite of one or two storm-signals (for example, the *nouvelle théologie*[1] and the almost anti-modernist sounding reaction in *Humani Generis*), ran slowly but steadily and boldly, with unavoidable crises, hesitations, and inadequacies, but without catastrophes: then this is the work – which could by no means have been taken for granted – of these men who pioneered that *aggiornamento* of the Church which began decades before the Council, received there its official ecclesiastical sanction and extension to the world, and of course is still far from reaching its end.

When something grows and changes without revolution, the growth and change always appear to be natural, as if nothing else could have happened. But how much patience, caution, resignation, trust, courage and humility, loyalty to the authentic tradition, tact, ability to wait without being cowardly and strength to begin again without revolutionary passion, were required to make it possible. These things were required from two aspects: in regard to the Church, in her ministry, in the unambiguousness of her teaching and the slowness of her growth, blessed and burdened by tradition; and in regard to the unchurched world with its wealth, its disruption, and its catastrophes, its estrangement from God while seeking the unknown God, as the Council itself described it. Among the men responsible for this growth and change Guardini is in the first rank. In the many-sidedness of his work, he might well be regarded as the very first of the German-speaking contributors to this *aggiornamento*.

We thank him at this moment of his death. We know that we are expressing the gratitude also of those for whom the Christian faith may not yet be at the centre of their lives, but who are nevertheless convinced that the maintenance of the human and eternal in man requires the dialogue of all men of good will: those who think therefore that honour and gratitude are due to anyone who can call across frontiers of estrangement and misunderstanding. Time today moves with terrifying haste. Hence it might seem that Guardini even before his death was hardly known to the younger generation, that his work had already passed into the anonymity of what is the German Church today. But even if this were so, his work would not have perished. And therefore today we still pay our grateful respects to this man who is now dead.

As we thank him in mind and heart for this work, we known that Guardini in the evening of his life felt the pain and thus the secret grace of knowing that his work had not been completed, of perceiving the uncanny speed with which history seems to move more than ever today and the impossibility of keeping up with it. But this only makes our gratitude more serious and profound. His work does not take away the burden of our own task or responsibility, from us who were permitted to live as his contemporaries and from the younger generation. But so too his work remains for us as an example and as a blessing. On him, however, we hope, eternal light is shining.

TRANSLATOR'S NOTE

1 The work of men like de Lubac and Congar before Rahner had begun to make an impact outside the German-speaking countries and long before what we have now become accustomed to call 'the new theology' began to take shape.

A MAN AT PLAY
PANEGYRIC FOR HUGO RAHNER

Like any human being, my brother Hugo was a man of contra-
dictions and he had to live with them. This was constantly evident
both in his life's work in theology and in his personal life. It seems
to me that his work, seen from outside, falls into three very
disparate sections: his patristic studies, his work on the life and
spirituality of St Ignatius of Loyola, his contributions to the theology
of proclamation. These three tasks which he set himself certainly
all arose from an inward inclination. He had an instinctive prefer-
ence for the historical as such and his 'theology of proclamation'
– which was far from being something taken for granted at the
time when it appeared – is the result of a positive joy in contacts
and of genuinely devout concern for his fellow-men of which the
letters of sympathy often provide moving testimony.

On the other hand, all this theological work constantly arose
also out of the casual situation which he took as his inspiration,
without grandiose plans and systems. In him the man always came
before the scholar. The inspiration of the moment outweighed the
long-term planning of a learned work. So, for instance, he gave
very important addresses at the Catholic Congresses in Vienna and
Cologne, the content of which was then truly 'progressive', and yet
he felt in himself no inclination for intellectual or ecclesiastical
politics. So too he took part in several Eranos-conferences and
thus established a close acquaintance with Carl Gustav Jung, but
he allowed himself to be pushed out of this circle comparatively
easily and unobtrusively.

His administrative abilities were certainly not outstanding, even
though he applied his gentleness and loving kindness in this field;
but at a difficult time he undertook for a year the rectorship of
the university of Innsbruck and for six years the rectorship of the
St Peter Canisius College: in these activities he was certainly no
worse (all things considered) than many other 'superiors'. Here too
he let himself be guided impartially by the concrete circumstances.

His main strength was in fact his devout humanness, which

was also the most distinctive feature of his scholarly work. It is not surprising that one of the best works is the small book *Man at Play*.[1] Or that in this patristic work he steeped himself lovingly in what at first sight might seem to be details of very secondary importance when and if they revealed something about man as eternal; or that he wrote a large and learned historical book on Ignatius and the women of his time. In the light of this joy in human contact it is possible to understand his inclination to play for years the part of something like a court chaplain to the Archduke Eugen in Igls and to be happy when moving in these circles, since he was loved everywhere for his singular combination of genuine and deep piety and an almost courtly wordliness, a talent for conversation with an almost inexhaustible fund of amusing stories and innocent jokes. But in these circles too he did a great deal of good and helped many to cope with life. He was, however, essentially a solitary person.

At the beginning of his life in religion he kept diaries of a touching youthful piety. I assume that he later burned them. At a later stage, even with me, he was silent about himself. This was particularly so in the last years of his terrible illness, which he described to his friend Alfons Rosenberg as a 'hell'. He deliberately gave up his work and his many close acquaintances. Fear, melancholy, and disappointment, the torment of a slow and consciously experienced bodily decay were not spared him. But even all this appeared in a form which seemed appropriate to him. His illness never lost its human shape and he had a quiet death. He accepted death willingly in faith and hope in the Lord whom he had tried to serve throughout his whole life. Apparently, in the last resort, without problems. But this very fact is perhaps the sign of a true Christian or at least one of the possibilities open to a Christian which means just as much as others. Karl Barth, who died not long before him and who on one occasion proudly showed him his own books and books written about him, once said that if the angels played before God they would play Bach, but among themselves Mozart. Hugo, the man at play, played his life more in Mozart's style than in Bach's. When he spoke, too, he could do so with spirit and enthusiasm. Pompous he could not be, nor did he give himself any particular airs of importance. But there was something behind it.

TRANSLATOR'S NOTE

1   Hugo Rahner, s.j., *Man at Play*, Burns & Oates, London 1965. This translation also includes a typical essay on 'Eutrapelia: a forgotten virtue'.

CONFIDENCE AND COMPOSURE
IN SICKNESS

Preaching God's word to the sick can be painfully embarrassing. The preacher himself is reasonably healthy, but has to speak to those who are not. He feels that they must be thinking: 'It's easy for him to talk. He's in good health.' Nor is it any help if he can say that he too has known serious illness. For he wasn't preaching when he was ill. And if he had been able to preach, he really doesn't know how he would have coped.

So all I can do at the beginning is to ask the sick to be ready to listen – even though they are not paid for it – almost in the same way as a traveller rightly looks at a signpost, notes its directions, and then leaves it behind him. The sick listener must also keep in mind the fact that illnesses are of so many kinds that it is almost misleading to speak of sickness in a general way. And yet, in speaking to the sick, it is impossible to address each one precisely with reference to his particular illness. For this reason too we are completely dependent on the benevolence and sympathetic understanding of the listener.

In the very last resort, the one whole life, in the midst and in spite of all the variety of things with which it is filled, is one single, great question, to be decided freely by each person: whether he will surrender himself trustfully and hopefully to the insoluble mystery we call God; whether he will entrust himself to it as to the holy, forgiving love which gives all things their ultimate meaning and gives itself to us.

Sickness is one of the events in which this one final question of life, which as such is always present, presses more clearly, is more rigorously stated, and demands our answer. For the sick person is or at least can be more lonely, he cannot so easily escape from the question which is really himself. His pain warns him of life's uncertainty; he is perhaps faced by the question which imminent death silently poses.

The sickness which a person experiences is not simply a fact, but also a task. We experience sickness itself as our own task, already fulfilled in one way or another, for good or ill, something

which we do ourselves and do not merely endure. We should not
merely react to sickness: this we have always done and the sickness which we experience in the concrete is always and already
that sickness out of which our own reaction to it emerges and
returns to us. It is a reaction of confidence and resignation in one,
or, also in one, a reaction of discouragement and distrustful
obstinacy, an insistence that we must remain healthy in absolutely
all circumstances. We should have confidence and resignation in
one. Confidence: that is, the will and the joyous hope soon to be
healthy again, because there are signs enough of this. But also
resignation, accepting sickness because we can mature through it
and because even death itself is not yet the end of hope and not the
triumph of that absurdity which we experience at the surface of life,
but blessing and grace. We should have both together: confidence
and resignation.

If a sick person is close to death, he might ask how he can
make his illness a task to be fulfilled with confidence and resignation, since his very situation means that he lacks the strength
of mind to do this: to preach this sort of thing to him is pointless
and to preach it to others, who do it without being told, is superfluous. It is true that, when our very last resources of mind and
heart are really beyond our control, our task ceases and anything
to be done about us and for us is left to the incomprehensible and
gentle power of God, so Christians believe, and we have nothing
more to do. But we can never capitulate in advance and claim
that we can do nothing more until we really have done everything
and have made the effort without considering whether we can
make it, but simply keep on with it. Fighting and not yielding, we
should let God's providence overpower us. As long as we are alive,
confidence and resignation in one should count as our task, to
which we devote all our strength even to the very last.

A part of our task in sickness is to remain always open to
others. Sickness can confront a person with himself in a fruitful
way. But it can also have the bad affect of making us selfish,
turning us back upon ourselves. It is a wonderful sign of the way
in which an illness can lead the sick person to maturity if, as a
result of it, he becomes kinder towards his own family, if he has
a cheerful word of consolation and interest for them and does not
merely expect others to speak to him in this way. Even a sick man
should make an effort not to take for granted the ministrations of

those who are nursing him, as if it simply could not be otherwise. He should practise towards those on whose ministrations he depends those virtues which otherwise make relations between people human and Christian: gratitude, politeness, attentiveness to the human being in the other with his own troubles, the nobility of mind which can generously overlook the faults of others, even when they are burdensome to ourselves and are imposed on us by those from whom we think we have the right to demand everything because we are ill and in a public hospital.

Most of what I have said up to now is perhaps open to the objection that I've been moralizing, and this is the last thing to do when talking to the sick. This may be true. But I think it is both hard and at the same time liberating to regard the sick person as open to an appeal, as capable of action, and to tell him that he can still give his heart in confidence, resignation, in love for the other, even in the midst of his distress, and, if he does so in God's grace, it will liberate him and alone make his sickness what it really ought to be.

After all that has been said, it still remains true that sickness cannot be understood, that it is a part of man's incomprehensible lot which is not solved by any commendation of its blessing or by any complaint. There are questions which are answered only by leaving them unanswered and accepting them. If we attempt to answer them in any other way, we are deceiving ourselves and making use of mendacious ideologies to produce a pain-killing remedy which does not sustain us for long.

Among these questions, which must be accepted in silence, is also serious illness. Why this and not another, why me and not you, why just now and not at another time, why so hard to endure while also exhausting our strength, why so cruel also to those for whom the sick person is concerned, why leading so close to death, why death, why ... ?

Such questions cannot be avoided, and there are no answers which can solve them. If a person accepts the questions hopefully and without despair, without (at present) expecting an answer other than that which is already implied inwardly and mysteriously in the persistent question, he is professing his faith in God and his love, whether he knows this or not. And someone who accepts this question is already participating in the life, sickness, and redeeming death of him who in dying said two words which only together – but truly so – hold already the whole destiny of man: the word acknowledging his being forsaken by God and the word that so gave his life into God's hands. The sick person who accepts the unanswered question lives by sharing in the life of Jesus, who cried on his deathbed, 'My God, my God, why hast thou forsaken me?', who knew (as the Epistle to the Hebrews says) that it is a fearful thing to fall into the hands of the living God – whose fearfulness overwhelms us at these very hours – and who nevertheless said, 'Father, into thy hands I commit my spirit.' Someone who lives with these two words of the Lord, who is sick and who, if God so decrees, dies, is in God's protection.

We are celebrating now the death of this Jesus who was so ill and died. Certainly the sick person has the right and duty to hope confidently that now his sickness will be overcome here and that he will get better. But, in order to fulfil the whole task which sickness puts before him, in order to know where the strength to fulfil it comes from, it is a good thing for the sick person to surrender himself, in a mysterious participation through this celebration, to the death of Jesus from which life came to be for us.

THE DOCTOR AND GOOD FRIDAY

At first sight, an article in a medical journal about Jesus' Good Friday* may seem odd. These brief reflections are certainly not meant to bring out the importance of the passion and death of Christ for our salvation in the sense understood by Christian faith and in the main article of faith of the Church's creed. Even though faith in the soteriological character of the passion of Jesus is decisive, in what the death of Jesus means to a Christian, this is not the place to develop and interpret the meaning of this faith. Here we shall merely attempt quite modestly to point to a couple of questions which may occur particularly to a Christian doctor in the light of his own calling when, as a Christian, believing, hoping, loving, he celebrates with the Church on Good Friday the death of our Lord as his own eternal salvation.

In the light of his calling and experience at deathbeds, the doctor will certainly think instinctively on Good Friday of the biological-medical aspect of the death of Jesus. In any case the Christian doctor is interested – not indeed only, but certainly particularly – in this aspect of the death of Jesus. With regard to this 'medical' question about the death of Jesus, two tendencies can certainly be distinguished in the literature and the devotion of Christians.

The medical facts

The first tendency attempts with the aid of the New Testament evidence to produce a medical picture of the death of Jesus as exact as possible. Before the physician, with his knowledge of dying in general and of the lethal consequences of a crucifixion, can have an idea as scientifically exact as possible of Jesus' dying and death, he must and ought of course also to have a picture as historically accurate as possible of what a crucifixion really was in Jesus' time. The same holds too for the scourging of Jesus which is part of the crucifixion – either as its prelude (as it mainly seems to be understood by the Synoptics) or merely as a fact (if it is understand as in John) – and was one of the causes of his

* See page 228.

death, particularly since a Roman scourging could often be itself the sole cause of death.

All these preconditions for a consideration of the death of Jesus from the standpoint of medical science, however, present considerable difficulties which cannot be expounded here in detail. Scourging can be carried out with very varying degrees of force (even if we assume as certain that Jesus was scourged in the Roman fashion and more or less in the way that was then usual as the prelude to an execution), and crucifixion took various forms which did not necessarily have a lethal effect in the same way. It must also be remembered that the principles of modern exegesis require us to be very cautious in dealing with particular historical statements or what occasionally only seem to be historical statements, since we always have to bring into our calculations also the 'literary form' and the theological intention in the gospel accounts (which holds particularly for John's account of the passion). For example, John's description of the water and blood flowing from the pierced side of Jesus is so much a theological interpretation that it can scarcely bear the weight of many medical hypotheses on the exact form of Jesus' death. In view of the fact that nailing was not then used for every crucifixion and in view of the peculiar literary character and late composition of John's gospel, which is the only one which clearly attests the nailing of Jesus to the cross (cf., however, Luke 24.39), we cannot perhaps claim with absolute historical certainty that the crucifixion took this form, although on the other hand there are no positive reasons for doubting that he was in fact nailed to the cross with four (not three) nails. The scourging, the nail-wounds, and particularly this unnatural hanging on the cross, produced the death of Jesus and in fact (by comparison with other reported crucifixions in antiquity) relatively quickly. In any case doctors are not unanimous about the exact and *immediate* cause of death (opinions and literature on this question are to be found in J. Blinzler, *Der Prozess Jesu* (3rd edn), Regensburg 1960, pp. 274-7. E.T. *The Trial of Jesus*, 1957, from first edition).

We shall have to say with Blinzler: 'It seems that the medical aspect of Jesus' death has not been finally clarified' (p. 276). In any case we should not draw any medical conclusions on the exact form of Jesus' death from what is known as the Turin shroud. The most serious suspicions about the Turin shroud (since Cheval-

lier) have not been cleared up, and it has also been used even in
our time to suggest that Jesus only apparently died. In the light
of historical science we can scarcely say more than that Jesus was
scourged and died on the cross. Beyond this, as historians and
physicians, we shall scarcely be able to say much that is certain
and exact.

Pious exaggeration

There is, however, another tendency in the ascetical and mystical
literature. For theological reasons an attempt is made to depict
Jesus' death as quite extraordinary and cruel beyond all other
deaths. This occurs both in the usual run of edifying literature and
also particularly in the descriptions of men and women visionaries.
The latter, for example, often claim to know the exact number of
blows Jesus received during the scourging. The basic scheme of
their recitals often consists in saying that God miraculously
heightened Jesus' capacity for suffering so that he could suffer
longer and more painfully than can be conceived or has in fact
happened in other cases. In fact, right into the present century
(for instance, by J. E. Belser, a Catholic exegete to be taken
seriously as such), the immediate cause of death has even been
sought in a miracle directly produced by God. This whole tendency
may be worthy of respect as a testimony to the piety of the authors
and the expression of their lively faith in the significance for
salvation of Jesus' passion, but it also leads to pure fantasies which
are theologically dubious and quite unhistorical.

Of course Jesus died the cruel death of crucifixion, of course
he freely took this biological death on himself, experienced it in
its depth and horror, and this experience was also affected by his
unique sensitivity. For *human* pain is always that of a person, who
is a unity of body and mind; it is not a merely biological phenomenon. But to go on from this to assert that even at the biological
level, as far as pain, etc., was concerned, the death of Jesus was
enacted in a way quite different from ours, and in particular from
other forms of violent death, is to assert more than is historically
proved and is theologically superfluous. I suspect that a doctor, in
the light of the history of cruelties up to the present time, could
imagine forms of death which he would regard at the biological

level as more atrocious than the death of Jesus – if there is any point at all in such comparisons.

Jesus became like us in all things except sin and, terrible as his death was, it was nevertheless the kind of death which has occurred thousands of times in history: what was really decisive in him was not the length and acuteness of biological pains, but his free acceptance of that destiny of death which belongs to every man and thrusts him into utter powerlessness. When the Christian, believing, hoping, loving, approaches the mystery of the death of Jesus, he does not need the visions of a Maria of Agreda or a Catherine Emmerich, for he knows all that he can and must know about it through the Church's creed which states that Jesus died on the cross for us.

A sublime example

It is precisely by understanding the death of Jesus not only as an abstract concept, but also in its concrete reality, as 'consubstantial' with our death, that our Lord's passion still remains a sublime and ultimately unique moral example (over and above its essential importance for salvation). There is a following and even an imitation (1 Cor. 11.1; 1 Thess. 1.6) of our Lord's passion (1 Pet. 2.20–4). But we should seek this imitation where Scripture especially places it: in his obedience in face of the terrible incomprehensibility of his lot as of God's will (Phil. 2.8), in the victory of powerlessness over power (to sum up in current terminology the content of 1 Pet. 2), in bravery against earthly powers even though this protest only leads to 'shame' (that is, 'social reprisals': Heb. 12.1–3; 13.2), in love of neighbour without fear even of death (John 13.34f with 15.12f).

The doctor and death

Laurens van der Post in his novel, *Flamingo Feather* (Hogarth Press, 1969, p. 14) speaks of a confrontation with death in this way: 'This man was an utter stranger to me, but in that look he was suddenly very close, as almost part of me, if only because we are in life all near to one another in our common nearness to this end which ultimately makes us one.' The doctor is present more frequently than others at the ending of a human life. And if he is a doctor and not merely a medical man, if he does not rush away even when he has been beaten by death in the struggle for this temporal life of the other person, if he remains as man and Christian though no longer as physician at this other person's end-point, then he will often see before him in this one man's destined death the doom of all mankind: of mankind of which he himself is part. He sees and experiences directly the closeness of his own death, death itself in its whole reality. For mankind is more than the multiplication and summing up of that abstract concept which we can acquire, according to scholastic logic, from our knowledge of an individual human being. And thus in the fate of the individual, and therefore also in his death, more can be perceived than a casual 'example' of what can happen to one individual. When we are present at the death of an individual, we are always also truly confronted with the event of the death of mankind.

The Christian, however, can interpret still more profoundly in the light of faith this mysterious unity in death, which confronts us in the death of the individual, the real unity, which is or ought to be the precondition and the immediate source of universal love among men. In Matthew 25 Jesus says that all we have done to the least of his brethren we have done to *him*. This does not mean the promise of an 'as if' which, in virtue of a moral-juridical fiction, gives to our actions a new valuation which has nothing at all to do with their intrinsic reality. For throughout all dimensions of human life there is really and truly a unity with the 'Son of man' who as God's word created the *one* mankind and himself truly shared in its history, since he became man even to the point of death on the cross. (We may interpret this unity philosophically and theologically as we like: it exists and is confirmed in that mysticism of ordinary life in which all meet the one who loves in a single individual.) Therefore on the one hand the destiny of the dying Lord is fulfilled only in the death of all men and, on the other, the doctor at the deathbed of any human being is standing in a mysterious truth before the cross of the dying Jesus.

What occurs in this death of an individual human being is not simply the 'same' as what 'also' occurred in the death of Jesus, but the particularity of an individual death (which also received the WORD of God) is burst open in the most radical way already in his incarnation and even more through the death of the God-man and spread into the one death of one mankind. That is why every death is an element in the death of Jesus: every death, in its very ordinariness, its wretchedness, in that powerlessness which mostly simply does not allow us to be 'heroic' at our passing.

The doctor at his baptism and in the Eucharist confronts the death of the Lord sacramentally ('mystically', Eutychius would say), but in his death and that of his fellow-men 'pragmatically', as the same Father of the Church says, adding that both forms belong together (cf. Karl Rahner, *On the Theology of Death*, 1961, p. 83). The doctor might try to say (varying a saying of Epicurus) that he has nothing to do with the *death* of the other, for he is concerned with this other person only as long as he is living and *as* a living man, and when the latter is dead the doctor is no longer interested in him. But if the doctor (as man and Christian) wanted to think in this way, he would not have understood Good Friday, he would be passing by his true life, the life of his fellow-men, the life of the Lord; he would be passing by the life that ends in death. On Good Friday we celebrate the death of the Lord *and* the holy death of mankind, which dies in the Lord (cf. Rev. 14.13). The doctor is serving this death even when he is fighting for man's earthly life.

6
Priesthood and
Religious Life in Upheaval

CURRENT DISCUSSION
ON THE CELIBACY OF THE
SECULAR PRIEST

AN ANSWER

You asked me to say something on the question of celibacy today at the conference of seminary rectors. What I can say should be regarded merely as a stimulus to your own discussion. The obvious reason for this is that it in the course of an hour it is possible to say only very little and to offer somewhat arbitrarily chosen remarks on a theme so difficult, so pressingly relevant today, and with so many strands. I am presupposing the continually increasing output of literature on the topic, my own letter on celibacy, and the Pope's encyclical, but I would like to admit honestly that I haven't studied all the literature closely. This will do no harm, since we are concerned here with the historical development of celibacy and of the obligation of celibacy in the Church and since, as a result of very many answers (positive and negative) to my letter on celibacy, I think I am fairly well informed about the questions which move the clergy today.

The question which seems to be directed at you as seminary rectors today amounts to this: Is your fight for celibacy merely the fulfilment of a legal obligation? Have we given up the fight inwardly as already lost? Are we also of the opinion that developments among the clergy and theology students have progressed so far already that sooner or later the legal barriers will be broken down, that pope and bishops will simply be unable to do anything else but abandon the law of celibacy? With regard to this question, it seems to me that everything depends on stating it correctly and then answering it in a personal decision which is something other than a shrewd calculation. The question must be correctly stated: that is, it may not be linked with an *a priori* defeatist, apparently shrewd prognosis of what will presumably come. A person who fights only when he is sure of victory has already lost. Someone who wants to fight only when he can see his way clear to do so in terms of this world, who assumes *a priori* that God is certainly

on the side of the big battalions, is not fighting in the right way.
We must also always consider whether we are to expect an early
victory or one in the more distant future. For the Church today
is living in a period of radical upheaval and of transformation
from a socially established Church of the whole people to one with
a few members who have made a wholly personal decision of faith.
If this Church is to be born in pain, the situation may well arise
when the question of celibacy will take a very different form from
what it does today.

The ultimate reason for the present crisis of celibacy

There are many reasons for the crisis of celibacy today. There
are those which lie in the modern social situation, those which
emerge from the mentality of modern man, those which have their
cause in the change of attitude to ecclesiastical authority on the
part of the individual Christian, those which are connected with
the nature of sexually conditioned human relationships and of
celibacy itself. But, if we are not deceiving ourselves, we must
see that the ultimate reason for the crisis by and large is to be
found in the present-day lack of faith. We are living at a time
when the reality of God and eternal life can be appreciated by man
only with difficulty. We are living at a time which is characterized
by catchwords like demythologization and secularization and by
the tendency to reduce the whole of Christianity to purely human
relationships.

The reasons for this situation, the way to face it, the new shape
of a Christianity which can find in it not only temptation but also
a kind of 'salvation', cannot of course be set out here. But it is at
once obvious, in a situation characterized by an apparent 'absence
of God', in which it seems impossible for man to realize his
relationship to the living God of eternal life, that the renunciation
in faith and hope of one of the highest and most central, albeit
intramundane, human values becomes a radical problem. In the
past too, of course, there were human tragedies and insoluble
problems. But formerly all this could in fact be undertaken in a
spirit of faith in the living God that was taken for granted, secure
in the faith that a sacred duty to God had been fulfilled, convinced as a matter of course of the impossibility of ever really

establishing an intramundane, successful harmony of life, bravely hoping for that eternal life in which alone all tragic situations, renunciations, and sacrifices find their solution.

This conviction, once taken for granted in the Church and in society at large, no longer exists. It has become difficult to renounce palpable happiness in this world and a direct experience of human fulfilment to which we can cling and which we can realize, for the sake of an eternal life which no eye has seen, no ear heard, and which has not penetrated any human heart. This is so much more difficult since, as Christians, we cannot in principle and least of all today simply set up as clear alternatives the desire for an intramundane future and human fulfilment, on the one hand, and the desire for eschatological salvation and the hope – verifiable to a certain extent – of eternal life on the other. Ultimately, then, the crisis of celibacy is a crisis of faith. This may not be clear to the individual priest or candidate for the priesthood in his personal consciousness, but it is a fact. Generally, this is passed over in silence or suppressed in the celibacy debate.

In defending celibacy to someone for whom it has become a problem and a life's crisis, we shall have to be cautious and make allowances for his particular situation, particularly since it is obvious that not every Christian has to face at the deepest level the problem of whether his faith can cope even with renunciation of marriage in the absolute hope of eternal life. But in principle we may not conceal the connection between the present crisis of faith and the celibacy crisis. It is our right and duty to state this connection clearly. We must ask the priest and the candidate for the priesthood today at what exact point in their life do those decisions exist, those real achievements, which so determine their life in the light of faith that this very life would be different if they did not believe in God and in eternal life. We must ask them whether their faith is merely a supplementary ideological super-structure, such that its loss or removal would not alter their concrete life at all; whether they *live* as if they had no hope, but at the same time cherish a hope which does not disturb them, does not change life, but only overclouds it a little, so that little would be lost if the hope turned out to be deceptive.

Of course this life-transforming realization of faith is a task required of every Christian, at least in the form of accepting life's tragic frustration and in hope of endurance of death. But there can nevertheless be no Christian life in which, in order to practise for that deed of faith which we do not control ourselves but is sent to us without our asking, a resolute approach to such a situation of life-transforming faith would be superfluous, a renunciation which is not forced from us but accomplished by us as a free act in the light of faith. If we see this essential connection between faith in eternal life and renunciation in general which alone transforms the folly of the cross and the hope of eternal life from an ideology into a reality of life, if we understand that the priest as witness and herald of the Christian faith must live out this renunciation which is the folly of the cross not merely through his word but through his deed, then we can ask the priest or the candidate for the priesthood whether he really believes and hopes when he yields to an understandable, human, and vital yearning and gives marriage an indisputable place in his scheme of life and bases on it his calculations in regard to everything else.

As such, there may be a thousand other ways in which a priest realizes this renunciatory deed of faith embodying a life's decision, through which alone he becomes a credible witness of the Gospel. He may approach martyrdom bravely, he may live in poverty, he may pledge himself to caring for lepers, he may risk his civic existence and even his life in protest against social injustice, he may wear out his life in selflessness without gratitude or recognition. But the folly of the cross and hope against all hope are a part of his life even today and still more tomorrow, and they mean something more and something more mysterious than that vocational commitment which can be expected of any social worker merely in the light of an intramundane rational calculation, if he is to do justice to his calling. If someone were to say that even a person of this kind will in the end be forced into the mystery of the cross and of the death of Christ, since this cannot be avoided in any human life, this merely confirms our thesis, as long as we understand that the Christian not only permits himself against all expectation to be overwhelmed by this mystery in his life but voluntarily approaches it, lets the bird in the hand (to express it in a banal way) fly away before it escapes itself or before the dove on the roof of eternity has already been caught. If, however, there is this understanding of Christian renunciation as an act really transforming human life through faith and this understanding of priestly life as testimony of faith, what objection can there be in principle to celibacy on the part of the priest who knows that he is called precisely to that concrete realization of faith which lies in celibacy? How could it be said that priesthood and celibacy, so understood, have no genuine intrinsic link with each other, although of course this does not mean *a priori* that they must by their very nature be necessarily linked with each other?

If we see and express the intrinsic correspondence between priesthood and celibacy as a concrete deed of faith, then the connection between crisis of faith and deed of faith is understandable: we have the right to ask the priest or the candidate for the priesthood whether he knows about this connection, whether he is aware of the radical nature of the commitment of faith, whether the crisis of celibacy for him is not a result of the fact that his faith is no more than the adoption, however humanly respectable, of a historical tradition the real nature of which he simply has not yet radically grasped.

Mechanisms of the arguments for and against celibacy

It may be a good thing to draw attention to a number of mechanisms and implications – for the most part unreflected and unexpressed – in the arguments for and against celibacy.

Celibacy more highly esteemed as a result of devaluing marriage
In the past there was certainly an argument for celibacy which flourished as a result of a devaluation of marriage, made sex taboo, suspect, and thus over-simplified renunciation of marriage as the higher way. The very fact of describing celibacy – as it has been described even up to the encyclical of Paul VI – as *castitas perfecta* implies that this dubious argument for celibacy is being invoked and a good deal of the arguments against celibacy gain their force from unmasking these false or irrational arguments on the other side. We must guard against this. But in fact we have no need of such an argument.

The higher the value put upon marriage, the more radically its importance for human life is seen, so much more radically can the point of its faith-inspired renunciation 'for the sake of the kingdom of heaven' be understood. The defence of celibacy does not gain its force from a devaluation of marriage. But we must not be so naive and unrealistic as to fail to understand what Paul in the first epistle to the Corinthians coolly observes: that marriage in the concrete can also be an obstacle to full surrender to the Lord and the task he sets before those who bind themselves to him and to the coming of his kingdom. Of course we can think of thousands of ministers of the word and thousands of priests who serve the Lord in his Church more joyfully and undividedly in marriage than thousands of unmarried, easy-going clerical bureaucrats who accomplish their ministry, satisfying their egoism both in it and outside it. But we should also not talk such nonsense as is found in some books on the subject, to the effect that a celibate is incapable of being a true brother to men, particularly to married men with families. This sort of stupidity is contradicted by the ordinary experience of any genuine priest who lets himself be used up as he puts his ministry at the service of men. We must coolly compare ideal with ideal, human inadequacy with human inadequacy, on both sides: then celibacy genuinely and sincerely lived in an attitude of religious faith has no need to fear these comparisons.

Purely verbal respect for the recognition
of renunciation of marriage in Scripture
It seems to me that the argument against celibacy is often conducted with a purely verbal respect for the recommendation in Scripture of the celibate life for the sake of Christ and the kingdom of God. There is even a tendency to cast suspicion on this recommendation in the Synoptics and in Paul as offending against the spirit of Jesus himself. For the sake of brevity, this will not be discussed here. But even when the charism of evangelical celibacy is recognized at least verbally, it seems to me, there is often little real understanding of this recommendation. Verbal respect is maintained to a certain extent in a subordinate clause, in order not to render one's own anti-celibatarian attitude suspect from the beginning as uncatholic and unchristian. But if we had a really genuine and lively understanding for this evangelical charism, much of the polemic against celibacy would certainly take a different form. Would we not then be obliged sincerely to regret the fact that understanding of this charism seems to be on the wane? Would we not then be bound to wish that the priesthood and this charism should be realized in the same person? Would we not more easily

discover an intrinsic harmony between these two life-styles? Would we not then point to the example of Paul rather than to that of Peter, the married man? Would not the example of Jesus then count more seriously also in this question?

A decision of practical reason

No one can defend celibacy on the basis of an absolutely essential and necessary connection between it and the priesthood. This is obvious, but the fact cannot be so easily exploited as an argument against celibacy when we remember that in the course of Church history there may be decisions freely made which then become irreversible, even though a different decision was possible at the time; the same is true of decisions made in the wider range of man's individual and collective history. When a selection is made between several possibilities, all morally lawful in themselves and open to the Christian, practical reason is involved. These are cases about which, from their very nature, we could go on arguing for ever.

Really there are here correct and weighty reasons both for and against a particular decision. But we do not then really argue in a way that fits the case merely by producing good reasons for one or the other decision and assuming that by this very fact we have established our position. Theoretical reason always remains dialectical and can never produce one decision as alone correct. There is always something in a decision which cannot be broken down reflectively and analysed into its constituent elements: it succeeds well only by resolutely surmounting the lasting problematic essentially involved in its theoretical substantiation. This need not mean a bad conscience, since the theoretical reasons cannot achieve that hundred per cent certainty which the decision itself must carry.

It is obvious that celibacy too, like every other decision in human life, can create hardships, frustrations, tragedies, in the individual case. This in fact is what life is about: anyone who wants to avoid these things always and in every case only gets involved in greater frustrations. In our case, moreover, it must also be clear that abolishing celibacy and replacing it with marriage for priests in the present mental and social situation would be bound to create quite new and very serious problems. What would have to be done about priests' marriages which break down? How would we deal with those personal claims which a wife today – as distinct from former times and from the situation among the married clergy of the Eastern Churches – rightly makes on her husband?

Arguments and objections against celibacy

In a third point we would like to enter into some arguments and objections against celibacy in itself and as ecclesially institutionalized for the secular priest. At the same time we are aware that we are thus placing ourselves on the defensive, which in itself is unfavourable to the cause of celibacy, because here too, from the psychological standpoint, attack would be the best form of defence. We must also be aware that a rational argument against the arguments and objections of opponents of celibacy cannot in itself alone break down emotional resistance to celibacy. Here too it is like trying to convince someone by philosophical and theological reasons of the goodness of God and the endurability of life when he has had the most terrible experiences of men's cruelty, the frustrations of human situations and death. The breaking down of such emotional resistance to celibacy, conditioned by painful experiences, demands more than these cool counter-arguments: living example, human readiness to help, and so on.

The psychological arguments
For the sake of brevity, we need not develop here the arguments against celibacy from the standpoint of psychology, of general anthropology, on the importance of the sexual factor for the maturing and the well-being of the human person. All this may be taken for granted, at least in theory. It cannot of course be denied that the results of these arguments from anthropology have not been sufficiently considered in the Church's theory and practice, and hence that there is still a great deal for the Church's teaching and practice to do to secure a genuinely human and healthy life combined with the endurance of celibacy; that much work has still to be done on many individual questions – for example, that of an uninhibited human relationship of the celibate to woman and even that of very concrete, moral casuistry; and that these things ought to be discussed without prejudice, although they used to be avoided as a result of nervous shyness and fear of taboo.

All this, however, cannot in any way change the basic fact that it simply is not true that celibacy necessarily leads to human frustration and neuroses, as long as the celibate is capable of it and called to it. Certainly there is in celibacy a renunciation of a central human value, marriage, and, if celibacy is not simply endured as a stubborn fate but freely chosen, a final justification is possibly only in the light of faith in grace, in the evangelical commendation of celibacy, and in an eternal life which surpasses all intramundane, human fulfilment. It is also obvious that celibacy does not lead to repression-neuroses, to compensatory actions and attitudes, only if it is really lived out as renunciation, which is something different from sullen repression. That there is a genuine possibility of celibacy, acceptable to common sense, has been expressly established, for example, by Albert Görres and Marc Oraison – that is, by really reliable experts. Always keeping in mind of course the conditions we have mentioned.

It should be emphasized once more that we need much more guidance and help than is generally provided in order to live celibate lives in a genuinely human fashion, not frustrating our human nature. Certainly there is still too much use made of fear and repression; we are still too far from seeing without inhibitions that even a celibate for the sake of the kingdom of God remains a man or a woman and that such people also meet, must and can meet, one another as people marked by sexual diversity.

None of this, however, should be allowed to prevent us from boldly and confidently rejecting a false or naturalistic anthropology, belittling human nature and leading us to feel that we have a bad conscience, that we are frustrated, crippled, afraid of taboos, or even homosexual. We know that we are sexual beings, we recognize the high value of marriage, we also see honestly all the dubiousness and perils of marriage in the concrete as a result of sin, but it is not for this reason or through fear of life that we give up marriage. We renounce it because it is possible to do so, because this renunciation can also imply a positive attitude to our own and others' sexuality, because it can be the concrete realization of our deed of faith, because there lies within it a freedom for undivided service to men in accordance with the testimony of the Gospel, because for various reasons there does exist in fact an inner convergence between celibacy and the priestly vocation.

Practical considerations

Such practical considerations are constantly raised, particularly in regard to the secular priest, and are felt to have a special urgency today. They are certainly not to be lightly dismissed. A continual heroism cannot be bluntly demanded of the normal secular priest: he too needs a place of security and relief from the cares of the daily grind. Today particularly it is difficult to provide this relief for the celibate. Where, for instance, will he find today a 'housekeeper' who is more – and she should be more – than a maid of all work with little or no education? How can it be managed today, even financially?

These and similar questions must be taken seriously. But when we allow for the fact that life, whatever we do about it, constantly and inevitably creates difficult and even tragic situations for which there is no ready-made solution, we may say that these practical difficulties of ordinary life can be solved on the whole in a humanly satisfying way, as long as there is good will, without abandoning celibacy. If in this connection the possibility of several priests living in community is suggested, the idea ought not to be rejected *a priori* as cold comfort or as Utopian. There are not a few signs that the evolution of pastoral work is tending towards a situation in which the custom of local parish priests living isolated from one another and alone will have become a thing of the past, when larger areas will be entrusted to the pastoral care of several functionally specialized priests working as a team. In the light of this, there appear to be greater possibilities for secular priests to live in community in the future than there are at present.

The argument based on legalized compulsion and the juridical institutionalizing of celibacy

This is certainly the most important argument against the celibacy of the secular priest. It is said that there may well be a charism of religious renunciation of marriage according to the testimony of the Gospel, but to couple this with the priestly vocation and make it a duty urged upon us by the Church and hedged about with legal sanctions is to contradict the very meaning of a free charism of individual celibacy for which we are responsible before God. In fact, this sort of thing contradicts also the individual's inalienable right to marriage.

In considering this argument, we are leaving aside for the time being the objection which should be discussed for its own sake: that there is a genuine vocation and aptitude for priestly pastoral work which should not be rendered impossible even if the person possessing it has no vocation or charism for celibacy. Leaving this aside then for the time being, in regard to the admittedly very briefly outlined argument, we must first of all decidedly and clearly insist that no one could have any legal claim to priesthood and ordination which could be asserted against the Church. If this claim does not exist, the Church may in fact confer the ministry and authority of priest on that person whom she selects in the light of an independent judgement. And she can make this selection dependent (presupposing of course that even so she can find a sufficient number of priests) on conditions which are appropriate in themselves and have a genuine if not essential connection with the priesthood. In principle, therefore, she can declare, without infringing the applicant's rights, that she will confer the priestly task and function only on someone who recognizes in himself the charism of celibacy and testifies before the Church that he is taking on celibacy in virtue of a free, personal decision and is determined to sustain it for a lifetime.

If it is said that most candidates for the secular priesthood would take on celibacy only as something not willed for its own sake, merely as decreed by the Church, a condition unwillingly endured for the sake of the priesthood which alone is positively willed, the answer is first of all that a quite elementary psychology shows that one out of two mutually dependent motives can still be genuinely chosen and realized if it is itself evoked by a more primary motive. Secondly, it may be asked whether it is really true that celibacy is considered and accepted even at the very beginning by the majority of candidates for the priesthood only as something to be endured against one's will, or whether this is only a later interpretation by the individual after the development of his priestly life has turned out unhappily, although it might have run differently. Thirdly, it must be stated forthrightly that a person may not accept ordination if he considers celibacy really as forced on him by the Church from outside as a condition for the priesthood, even though he sees no intrinsic and positive connection between the two.

We must, however, consider further the argument based on the idea of a legalistic enforced celibacy. On this it must be said that it is not true that a God-given personal charism in the Church cannot be a reality in the public life and in a sacral-legal area of the Church. This whole way of arguing against the institutionalizing of charismatic celibacy arises from an ecclesiology which interprets the institutional factor in the Church in the light of the model of a secular society and thus comes to the conclusion that everything institutional in the Church must be shaped in such a way that it is independent of existential resolution, of grace and charism, and on the other hand that the charismatic element must be kept free from all directives and all institutional elements in the Church. But this is an ecclesiological error, the result of a failure to understand the mysterious nature of the Church.

It is precisely in her social palpability, in the juridical dimension of her sacraments, in the sacral-juridical order of her life, that she is herself the incarnatory manifestation of grace, of charismatic holiness, and of the personal decision of faith. This has been her understanding of herself from the beginning. The free, charismatic breathing of the Spirit itself she has also always fitted into an order, and this very order she regards in turn as the incarnation of her spirit; she has never seen her order as something coming from outside, alien to the spirit and oppressing the spiritual element within her. The Church is well aware that law – whether divine or merely human is irrelevant – does not become a spur to sin, the occasion of unfreedom and death, only if it is inwardly filled by God's grace in the freedom of the children of God; but she has always known too that she can approach men and make demands on them with this law on her lips in order to appeal to the power of the Spirit which God offers to man to enable him to fulfil the law and elevate it into the freedom of an inward 'must' and 'can'; she has always known that this very power of the Spirit, as hoped for and presupposed as given in hope, is manifested in her visible life, which also has a juridical structure. If this is denied, then, to be logical, the Church's power to bring into a juridical order the charismatic life of those whom we call 'religious' would also have to be questioned.

It may readily be admitted that the very constitution of the secular priest's life also includes an element of that sacral-juridical and – for that very reason – spiritual way of life which is followed from the very beginning and in a recognized way in the public life of the Church by religious orders and particularly today by secular institutes. This factor is of course not necessarily involved in the life of the secular priest. But if we were to deny in principle that it can and may be there, we would also have to raise an objection in principle to the sacral-juridical organization of the life of celibacy, poverty, and obedience in the Church: this would be to destroy the true nature of the Church and reduce it in the last resort to a secular society, to the visible Church of a mere religious organization on the one hand and the absolutely invisible Church of the Spirit and of grace on the other. But both have found precisely in the incarnatory Church of Christ an indissoluble unity eschatologically assured by God's grace, so that the spiritual element must find in the visible Church an institutional palpability which makes the historically experienced concreteness of that Church a testimony and a manifestation of the Spirit irrevocably promised to her.

During the Church's pilgrimage, spirit and internal impulses on the one hand and letter and law on the other can never be made to coincide in a blessed harmony, but neither can this often tragic distinction be overcome by tearing them apart. The Church and, in the last resort, only the Church can have the courage to say, 'You ought', because she can say in virtue of God's mission, 'You can, for you possess the grace to do so in my socially constituted community of the Spirit.' This she can and may do also in regard to the celibacy of those who have acknowledged before her the charism of virginity. This no more implies that 'you can' is said here with an absolute certainty than on any other occasion when the Church says, 'You ought and you can' in a human being's concrete situation, since the Church cannot make a final judgement on the concrete human being; but this impossibility does not dispense her from addressing the concrete human being in this way.

It is of course correct that the Church in the light of this must consider again and more precisely for the future what is to be her reaction in the concrete to the person who later says, 'I can't' or 'I can't any longer'. It is, however, false to assert that the Church is wrongly legalizing the charism of celibacy when she reminds a priest that he took this on himself for life. This counter-argument of course presupposes that a person may bind himself by a free decision to a way of life which he cannot simply abandon later, at his own whim and discretion, without breaking an important obligation. But the possibility of such morally irreversible decisions by a person mature enough to make them cannot be disputed in principle.

Entry on a life-long marriage is a genuine example of this, in spite of the way in which opponents of celibacy reject the parallel. The example does not lose its force because of the fact that in the one case there is the acceptance in a free decision of something that belongs to natural law, in the other a charismatic vocation (not merely a law of the Church). If in fact the free acceptance of the obligation to a permanent way of life under certain conditions were by its very nature contrary to man's freedom and to the unforeseeable historicity and mutability of a human existence, then a human being could not be expected to bind himself even in regard to marriage. But if the latter is a genuine human possibility in principle and in general, then the same kind of possibility exists in regard to celibacy. To reject this would involve also the rejection *a priori* of life-long vows in a religious order as immoral. Of course, in the light of this we might also point out that the Church, in regard to dispensing from priestly celibacy or, perhaps better, in regard to recognizing an individual's experience of being no longer bound before God by this personal decision made in the past (an experience which certainly cannot be rejected in principle as impossible), should not proceed more rigorously than she does when dispensing from life-long vows religious who are not priests. We can say this at least when, on the one hand, we do not forget the separability in principle of priesthood and celibacy and, on the other hand, we remember, in spite of the 'indelible character' of the priesthood, that the laicization of a priest – even apart from the question of celibacy – must not be regarded in every case as something which can be the result only of moral failure.

The argument based on the possibility of a personal vocation to pastoral work without the charism of celibacy

It is often said that there are many today who, in virtue of their intellectual and human qualities and by their deepest inclinations, feel called to the pastoral work of a priest, indeed patently more so than many who are prepared to accept celibacy, but are not aware of any charism of this kind in themselves and have decided on marriage. It is said that it is precisely the best who leave the seminaries, because of the obligation of celibacy, while those who are less worthy, immature, and dull, remain. But this is to the detriment of souls, spoils the image of the priest, produces a negative selection, and leads to an increasing shortage of priests.

On this it must be said that if the Church really cannot find clergy in sufficient numbers and with adequate qualifications, as long as the law of celibacy remains, she will have to abandon celibacy at least where this situation holds. This is a question of fact which will be dealt with later. For the time being, however, it must be said that talent and disposition for priestly pastoral activity are not sufficient in themselves to constitute a vocation to the priesthood, nor do they establish a legal claim on the Church to the priesthood. Apart from a real call to the priesthood by the Church, there is no absolutely specific talent or disposition for pastoral activity only capable of being fulfilled through the priesthood itself which could justify a moral claim on the Church to ordination. Such dispositions and talents, which are by no means to be disputed, can be fulfilled in other callings and ways of life, so much the more as it becomes clear in the modern theology of the priesthood that the latter contains a whole complex of ministerial functions in the Church which are by no means necessarily found or must be exercised merely within the official priesthood. Furthermore, particularly for the future, we ought to expect and strive for a greater specialization and differentiation of ecclesiastical, even institutionalized ministries, which do not by any means have to be identical with what we understand today to be the content of the official priesthood or even the diaconate and which nevertheless can and should have an important, officially recognized place within the one and whole ministry of the Church.

If these opportunities were seriously and boldly grasped the Church could make use of the services of many people with such dispositions and vocations, without simply putting them under the control of the priests. At present they are often faced with the harsh dilemma either of taking on themselves a celibacy they don't understand or of renouncing service for men under the official mandate of the Church. In the light of this we ought to reconsider, for example (and it is only an example), the question whether married theologians might also act for the Church as university professors. A bishop might also use his creative imagination to discover other concrete ways of making use in the Church of such talents and dispositions. And again this must not necessarily mean the exercise of an auxiliary function in subordination to the clergy (in the present-day sense of the term). The arguments cited here against celibacy therefore do not prove that there cannot be a group of holders of particular functions within the one and whole ministry in the Church who also by celibacy bear witness to the faith they proclaim.

Shortage of priests

The shortage of priests is also said to be the result of imposing the obligation of celibacy and is therefore used as an argument against it. This argument must certainly be taken seriously, but we may ask whether it proves clearly and in the concrete circumstances of a larger area of the Church what it sets out to prove. It is certainly true, as we have already frequently pointed out, that if the Church cannot in fact find a sufficiently large number of priests for a wider area without giving up the obligation of celibacy, then she must take this step. For the obligation of providing according to her resources for a sufficiency of pastoral clergy is imposed on her as a divine precept; but the same cannot be said for maintaining the obligation of celibacy. But the question is, at least with regard to European conditions, whether abandoning celibacy would really increase the numbers of the clergy, particularly in the long run: in other words, whether the obligation of celibacy is actually and also for the future the cause of the shortage of priests.

It should be made clear from the start that this question of the necessary or desirable number of clergy itself involves a further question. It is in fact not so easy to say just how numerous the priestly ministers ought to be. This is a difficult question, both when we recall that many functions which today are in fact exercised by priestly ministers are by no means necessarily or for ever part of their ministry, and also when we ask how the desirable percentage of priests among the churchgoing people should be decided: should it be settled simply in the light of the numbers of the population, as in the people's Church, or according to the numbers of those who are really personally and genuinely believers, as in a community Church (allowing of course for a number of extra priests for missionary work to the now pagan surrounding world).

Even if we leave aside this question, which is by no means easy to answer, the problem of the connection between the shortage of priests – which we shall here assume as a fact, although with some reservations – and the requirement of celibacy can also be answered only with difficulty. In the first place we see that there is the same shortage of recruits for the Church's ministry even in the Protestant Churches where married pastors are taken for granted. The abandonment of celibacy is therefore certainly not a panacea for the shortage of priests. Nor can it be denied that there are today, perhaps, a not inconsiderable number of young Catholic men who would become priests if there were no obligation of celibacy. But it must nevertheless be asked whether this situation will persist.

If we try to understand more exactly the type which exemplifies what is particularly characteristic of these young people, we shall certainly find not a few whose personality structure – quite apart from the question of celibacy – presents, if we may so express it, an oddly mixed fabric. On the one hand, they came from a still existing Christian and churchgoing milieu which is more or less taken for granted; questions and ideals related to an outlook on the world, a life within a Christian and churchgoing circle, are still for them to some extent a part of a social background that is taken for granted, but they are a long way from accepting these things adequately and bringing them to bear on a personal decision which will enable them to face a hostile environment. On the other hand, they are children of our age, supremely critical and inwardly disturbed in regard to the traditional understanding of faith and the time-honoured Christian life-style, and particularly allergic to established ecclesiastical authorities. In the light of this second constituent of this oddly mixed type – that is, of a world with supremely personal claims to palpable happiness, to human security and so on – it would scarcely occur to them to adopt a positive attitude to the charism of celibacy, particularly when it is presented to them in the form of a requirement of the Church.

This oddly mixed type therefore includes also precisely those young men who want to be priests, but are not prepared to give up marriage on this account. It is the counterpart of the modern Church as a mixed type between the traditional people's Church and the slowly growing community Church of personal believers, largely independent of a disappearing Christian milieu. This oddly mixed type of young person is therefore definitely a transitional phenomenon which we certainly cannot expect to continue into the more distant future. But then the question arises: Shall we in future, in the light of the number of members of the future community Church, not have a sufficient number of priests without abandoning celibacy, if by that time candidates for the priestly ministry will almost without exception be men whose personal decision for faith and priesthood will no longer be influenced to anything like the same extent as formerly and today by traditional Christianity, taken for granted with its own kind of Church loyalty?

I wouldn't venture to answer the question with any certainty one way or the other. But I can imagine that the future decision of faith on the part of young people in the midst of a secularized society will be sustained by such a solitary determined opposition to the environment, by such a nonconformity, that the result will be a wholly new attitude to celibacy, to some extent taking it as a matter of course. These people of the future will no longer feel that the priesthood is a calling which is simply part of the structure of bourgeois society for which people decide almost as they decide to be doctors or teachers. This decision will be felt as typically nonconformist, as a decision for a way of life which is of its nature opposed to what is otherwise customary, for a life which will be poor and unconventional, which will no longer be financed by a church tax collected by the state, a life without the social status attached to academic distinction.

I can imagine that anyone who resolves on such a priestly life in future will also decide, almost without more ado, for celibacy. If it were to be said that decisions of this kind involve the prospect of a small number of priests, we may certainly ask whether it would be any greater under the conditions which are inevitably coming even without celibacy; we may also ask whether the small number of clergy in the future will not be just as effective (within the scope of what is possible) as the present-day clergy who bear undoubtedly bourgeois features in marked contrast to their task of proclaiming the gospel of the cross. We may wonder, then, whether the argument against celibacy based on the shortage of priests is not unconsciously affected by a situation which still exists today but will no longer exist tomorrow, and fails to envisage a future situation which will once again demand in a completely new way the celibacy of the priesthood.

The argument based on statistical investigations

In Holland, in the U.S.A., and elsewhere opinion polls have been organized which are supposed to elicit information about the attitude of the clergy, particularly the younger clergy, and candidates for the priestly ministry to the obligation of celibacy. In Germany too similar attempts have been made, but of a more private character and on slighter basis. It is understandable that such an existential and intimate question as that of one's attitude to celibacy is scarcely a suitable object for investigations of this kind, and it is not entirely surprising that Rome tries to get the bishops to prevent these surveys and particularly the publication of their results. But whether such efforts are tactically prudent or render suspect the determination of the higher ecclesiastical authorities to maintain celibacy is another question; we realized at the Council how difficult it was.

However that may be, the results of these inquiries have a certain signifiance, but they must be properly understood and correctly interpreted in human and theological terms. The conclusions certainly provide information on a number of items: whether the effort to gain understanding for the charism of celibacy among priests, candidates for the priestly ministry, and also among the educated laity, has been successful enough; whether we have not neglected a lot or acted wrongly in this respect; whether education in the seminaries took the right course; whether the effort on the part of the Church's authorities to promote a concrete life-style for priests, helpful to the celibate, was adequate; whether the distribution of the Church's ministry and the use of lay people for the tasks of the institutional Church was undertaken boldly and in the right way; and so on. These surveys may also provide some indication as to whether a sufficiently large number of clergy can be expected in the future without giving up celibacy. But such inquiries and 'polls' have also their serious limitations.

The history of the Church itself teaches that the Holy Spirit must not always and necessarily be on the side of a purely numerical majority, that the Church has the right in certain circumstances – even against very deep and widespread growing trends – to utter a harsh 'No', although this does not mean that leaders in the Church need do no more in such situations of conflict than appeal to their formal authority, which can easily be overstrained, and then simply issue a prohibition. Even the institutional Church has the duty, without overstraining its formal authority, to provide a lively defence of its case and to see the question of celibacy particularly in a wider context, in which alone it can be given a genuine and convincing answer. But the situation may also arise in which the higher authorities in the Church have the duty of reminding those who have undertaken the priesthood in a free decision, humbly but also seriously and trusting in the grace of God, of the sacred decision for life which they made freely at the beginning of the priesthood; they have the duty of asking candidates for the priestly ministry forthrightly whether they are aware of the charism of celibacy in themselves and, if not, to tell them that they are not called to the priesthood as it is conferred in the Latin Church.

Incidentally, it is quite another question in what genuinely human and intrinsically respectable way the Church should charitably release from her service those priests who have reached the conclusion after ordination that they can no longer fulfil the obligation of celibacy in a way compatible with human dignity. In this respect there are certain formulations even in the encyclical of Paul VI which are not entirely happy: the old practice was certainly often inhuman and therefore unchristian, and was based on presuppositions which are not beyond question, and the new practice also is presumably only a transitional phenomenon.

As we already said, the defensive position adopted in these reflections is perhaps not very favourable to the cause of celibacy. The positive theological evaluation of celibacy and of its convergence with the priesthood – which exists despite all objections, in regard both to the priesthood as such and also to the concrete priesthood of the future – was inevitably inadequate. The impression might even have been created that celibacy has been taken too much for granted as an unchangeable fixed point in the light of which everything else has been dialectically determined and reduced to a status in which it cannot be used as a serious argument against celibacy.

It cannot be disputed that such a method has its dangers, that (to put it quite crudely) once we have secretly decided on something, the reasoning intellect always produces the necessary arguments. But there is the same danger in the anti-celibacy position. Here too it is possible, secretly and without reflection, to be already against celibacy in virtue of a basic decision the motivation of which has by no means been thoroughly considered: then, of course, a sufficiently large number of really obvious reasons are found for that position. With regard to such basic decisions affecting the whole of human life, if we are honest, we simply cannot argue from a methodically absolutely neutral position. The relation of this obvious epistemological fact to total (ecclesial and individual) existential decisions should not be concealed by either of the parties. Nevertheless there may be a possibility of a 'discernment of spirits' which need not be based on a completely adequate reflection.

We may wonder: Where does the decision occur in virtue of that faith which is folly and scandal to the world, in virtue of a theology of the cross, in virtue of a faith which knows that the loveliest things of the world and of human life have to go through the zero point of death in order to stand before the God of eternal life and to be able to be brought into his eternal kingdom? If we put this question bluntly to ourselves, then, I think, we have taken up that standpoint of the Spirit and of faith at which we know how our question must be answered; or, to put it more cautiously and modestly, we know what it is to which we have to bear witness and for which we have to fight in the Church, with the quiet assurance that, when we have done what is our duty, God himself will so direct the history of his Church as he – and not we – knows and wills.

THE MEANING AND JUSTIFICATION
OF PRIESTLY CELEBRATIONS

Let's face it, right from the beginning: priestly celebrations are 'a problem'. At one time the finest and greatest buildings to be seen were churches and, to some extent, state residences and offices, but now it has become quite impossible for these to compete with other handsome structures and therefore no one feels any urgent need to build magnificent churches. It is the same today with priestly celebrations.

For many reasons they have ceased to be taken for granted. We are reluctant today to show and still more to organize 'religious feelings'. We no longer react so devoutly to the clergy, we don't distribute laurels in advance (at a priest's first Mass) so gladly and spontaneously. The image of the priest – allowing for all consistency in dogma, which of course must be thought out afresh – is no longer so unambiguous in terms of the sociology of ideas and of society that it is easy to say on these occasions just *whom* we are feasting.

We used to be more naïve. We planned a feast for someone who came equipped with higher, mysterious powers from above into the midst of a secular people, but who was thrown back on these powers: he came as the bringer of salvation, as the reverend father, to whom (as Archbishop Katschthaler expressed it in the ninteenth century, when preaching at a first Mass, to the horror of the Protestant theologian Mirbt) God has given power over God himself. Nevertheless, we shall have to say that all this still implies something very true and Catholic.

Change in the Christian mental horizon

First of all, however, we have an uneasy feeling, particularly today, that we just cannot stand celebrations of this kind any longer. This is not to say that what we used to celebrate did not exist. But we may say without hesitation that behind the celebration was an horizon of understanding and experience which is past, which was not even really Christian, but pagan. This was possible because nothing at all was said or asserted, but tacitly and implicitly presupposed. The mental horizon was defined by the difference between the secular people below – the laity – and the priest equipped with heavenly powers above.

If we want to confirm this, we need only ask whether, at the celebration of a priest's first Mass in the old style, there was ever any mention of the fact that there is a holy Church of which all are members; that there is a holy people of God equipped with divine gifts and mission, a priesthood of all; that the layman is not merely the recipient of the priest's activity, but has likewise an active role in the Church which is important also for the priest, while the latter also as such lives on the spiritual dignity and mission of the so-called layman just as the layman lives on the priest's gifts. I don't think that these things were mentioned at priestly celebrations of the old style. But this must be the horizon of understanding and experience of such celebrations today, if they are to continue at all.

This change is necessary, not because we have become more 'democratic', more sceptical in regard to the clergy, more laicist or anything of that kind, but because the true mental horizon is not the ultimately pre-Christian, pagan difference between the secular from below and the sacred from above, but something specifically Christian, the holy Church herself of all men. In this case too we can see what can otherwise be observed in the history of the Church, of dogma, of piety: what is Christian enters first (it is not possible otherwise) into a still pre-Christian horizon of understanding (concepts, ideal types, perspectives, etc.), is first expressed clearly enough under these presuppositions, but then slowly transforms this horizon of understanding itself. If we presuppose this transformation, there can and may – indeed, there should – be priestly celebrations also in the future, since they are then given their rightful place and take a form appropriate to their true meaning.

Celebration and feast

Before we go on further, however, from what has really now been established as the starting point of our reflections, there is still

something else to be said. People today have not much of a capacity
for celebration. For the most part they are much inclined to bring
home in a solemn form the real depth of what they are doing
in ordinary life, to give it a certain radiance in order to accept more
consciously and decisively what they are and the prosaic reality
of what they are doing. They feel that weddings where the bride
has a magnificent dress and the guests turn up in limousines are
old-fashioned and strange, that great solemnities of state are hum-
bug, that solemn funerals with doleful speeches and mountains of
wreaths are merely embarrassing attempts to cover up the bleak-
ness of the end.

When modern man tries (and perhaps has a greater need today
than formerly) to break through the grey, institutionally manipulated routine of ordinary life, with its strict assignment of roles in
society, he does not ask for a heightened solemnity to be given
to his life – which is in fact properly his and must be accepted as
such if he is not to become 'schizophrenic' – but wants to break
out wildly and seek a complete contrast to the strict routine and
the iron rule of the ordinary life of duty. He runs to the dream-
world of the cinema, to the anonymity of the tourist far away from
home, to the mad riot of the carnival where a different 'morality'
holds, and so on.

And yet there must be festive celebrations – that is, the public
and social manifestation of what constitutes the actual truth and
reality of existence, the intentional public elucidation of what man
is. This would be superfluous if man were undialectically always
simply what he should be and is. But man must become, first of
all by his acceptance and decision, more and more what he is.
He must seek and overtake himself. He comes to be only by keeping
before himself what he wants to be. And if and because he is at
the same time a social being in all the dimensions of his existence,
this solemn manifestation of the otherwise grey and almost always
ambiguously realized existence in ordinary life must in fact bring
out publicly the meaning of this existence in its great powers and
tasks, particularly when what has to be solemnly expressed is
itself a factor of man's own social nature.

Hence, in spite of all the scepticism with which modern man
regards himself, feasts are celebrated even today. We turn births
and birthdays into feasts, make a solemnity even of burying a
corpse, celebrate marriages, celebrate state receptions: the head

of the state makes solemn public appearances (which seem somewhat superfluous), receives the diplomatic corps; parades take place, youth-dedications are devised; swearing-in ceremonies, openings of term, taking office, are made into festive occasions: in a word, festivities cannot be eradicated. And even the most rationalistic technocracies, which are really supposed to have no time for such essentially superfluous celebrations, retain the old and sooner or later devise new ones, even if they are only magnificent receptions for astronauts. It is better and more honest to acknowledge in theory what we do in fact: celebrate feasts. In this way we profess the courage to speak with praise and gratitude of what in fact is, rules, and operates in man's existence, although it seems to be buried in the always ambiguous routine of ordinary life, only too often betraying what is most real – although this happens and just because it happens.

Celebrating Church

In this sense the Church too must celebrate feasts. For her nature and her task are very closely related to human existence, since she is a socially constituted *community*. In the light of this, of course, her most authentic celebrations, in which she brings her own nature before herself and before her constantly renewed decision of faith, are not 'priestly celebrations' but the feasts properly so-called of the Church's year and particularly Pentecost. This is true if only because she has to reflect first and last, not on herself, in order to remain aware of herself, but on the deeds which God himself does in Jesus Christ (what he does of course always to the world and to her, so that her meaning is also brought out in *all* feasts).

Eucharistic celebration

She may, however, without hesitation go beyond these main feasts. And consequently, in a secondary way, she may also recall solemnly in greater detail what she is. And this includes also her ministerial priesthood. Something of the kind occurs at the eucharistic sacrifice on some days when I add my own petition for the Pope and the bishop. Feasts of saintly popes and bishops are also included, since God is thanked in them really for the achievement of unity between the institutional and charismatic elements in the Church; this can be extended beyond such properly liturgical feasts to what are considered in this book as 'priestly celebrations'. In this respect no harm is done if such celebrations go beyond what is strictly liturgical. There are two reasons for this. In the first place, the less strictly cultic features of such celebrations in particular emphasize the dissociation of the 'object' of the celebration from the Church's central realities of salvation. But, secondly, in the 'secular', 'human' elements of such a celebration it is made clear to some extent that the Church's reality extends beyond the dimension of profession of faith, of the sacrament, and of cult as such.

The real altar-community presupposes, demands, and produces (of itself) a community of people who believe, hope, and love, which is also 'human' and 'natural': neighbourliness, brotherliness in ordinary life, charity in all forms, which are required by a particular time and situation, the will to integrate the often so helpless individuals into a genuinely human community. That is why a Christian local and altar-community would not be completely real if it became visible *only* at the altar in cult, profession of faith, and sacrament, leaving its members afterwards to go their separate ways back into the anonymity of the present-day secular mass-society. The altar-community may not be a ghetto-like, 'closed society' of a sectarian character, but neither may it be *only* a liturgical altar-community. By the fact that it is more, it can be known whether it is a genuine eucharistic community, in which *that* unity of the faithful in Christ is celebrated which is only really achieved in ordinary life, in practical love which 'those of the household of the faith' particularly owe to one another. What, superficially regarded, seems to be the secular, 'social' element of a priestly celebration can thus make clear and help to realize precisely that dimension of brotherly neighbourliness in a local community which also belongs to the essence of the local Church.

Priestly celebration and priesthood

Such a priestly celebration today, however, must take a form which corresponds to the reality celebrated and to the justified mentality of the present time. Thus we return to the position reached already at the beginning of these reflections. It should really be obvious that a priestly celebration, for all the human warmth it naturally generates, holds properly not for a particular priest but for the priesthood.

We certainly don't have to discuss specially here the consequences of this fact in regard to what must be done and particularly what must be omitted, all the less so since in this respect the right note will be struck only when everything is done with tact, modesty, spontaneity, and sensitivity, and since the mentality, educational level, number, and so on, of those who are included in such a celebration vary considerably. What is more important is to see the priesthood itself correctly in the celebration. And this means: in the light of the Church as one and whole. That is not to say that differences in the function which a person exercises in the Church should be effaced or minimized. Why should they? If there is a celebration for someone taking office in a secular society, the person who does not hold such an office does not feel that his dignity is lowered or his social prestige affronted. What belongs to the priesthood should be given expression and acknowledged. This is in accordance with the truth of faith. And when the believer who does not belong to the ministerial priesthood hears of it and acknowledges it, he is referring only to what exists to serve him. It should also be said without hesitation, forthrightly and without prejudice, that the function and authority of the ministerial priesthood comes from Jesus Christ and is intelligible only in the light of this fact.

This ministerial priestly authority, however, must first of all be so understood and described that (as Franz Xaver Arnold puts it) the difference between mediating and achieving salvation remains clear. This again means two things. Firstly, the priest does not stand 'between God and man' (a projection which is very dangerous and in the epistle to the Hebrews is applied to Jesus Christ, not to the ministerial priesthood) in such a way that the Christian's immediacy (in grace, prayer, the call of conscience, charisms, etc.) to God and Christ is removed. The priest is not an intermediate member in a succession of authorities over grace itself, but (as far as his function extends) the 'instrumental' minister of the incarnatory (sacramental, social) *manifestation* of grace (admittedly, an effective, productive manifestation) which links man immediately with God: minister of the sign of grace which gives what it signifies only when the person in whom it is realized is immediately related to God, in order to accept as his own the grace signified in faith, hope, and love. And thus, secondly, the difference between mediating (in preaching and sacrament) and achieving salvation, which is not to be obscured in commending the authority of the ministerial priesthood, implies that all the salvation-mediating activity of the priest does not relieve the Christian of his task of achieving himself his unity with God in the grace of Jesus Christ in his own existence right down to the routine of ordinary life.

Christianity does not consist merely in what the priest does for the Christian, in Church and preaching, in the Eucharist and in administering the sacraments. The ministerial priestly function must be understood in the light of the *whole* reality of the Church. Celebrating the ministerial priesthood must not lead to the old error of supposing that the Church is first of all simply the clergy and that the laity are merely the object of clerical activity. Because there is a Church, there is office in the Church. Because there are those who believe in Christ, because there is the royal priesthood of all who are baptized and justified, because these are all united to the body of Christ, there is a Church. And because *this* Church is and should be both community and society, there must also be 'office' in her. And this office has its function, its dignity, its limits from *this* Church.

That is not to say that it derives its mandate and its authority 'democratically' from the sum-total of individuals in the Church. Its mandate is derived from the fact that God in Christ has willed and loved this Church and in this will for this Church also wills and constitutes the necessary office in her. It is not necessary to discuss this theme further here (cf. Karl Rahner, *Das Amt in der Kirche*, Freiburg 1966). But it must be clearly seen if we are to talk about the priesthood objectively and opportunely on the occasion of such a celebration.

None of this need detract from the joyful celebration of the ministerial priesthood. In the last resort it is quite superfluous in this justified and necessary celebration to rack our brains about or to concentrate on what the ministerial priest 'alone' can do (for instance, to insist, as it was formerly customary to insist at a priest's first Mass, that he alone can 'consecrate' or 'absolve'). For even in what is 'reserved' to him alone he is the servant of the holy community, and it is so reserved as assigned to him really by Christ, but reserved only in so far as it occurs in an 'orderly' way according to the will of God: hence it is really given to the Church as one and whole and not a large number of isolated individuals. Just because all that has been given to the priest was given to him for the sake of the Church and in him to the Church, what is given to the Church can be said without prejudice also of him when celebrating the grace of his mandate, without trying anxiously to work out whether it is given to him alone.

We can do this simply because he has already done most of what pertains to his office merely by doing what the Christian must do, because what is special to his office 'alone' calls him afresh precisely to be a Christian; because (as distinct in many ways from men in many other callings) he exercises his office rightly only by involving in it his whole Christian existence. If we say, then, that he must be simply a brother among brothers and sisters, one who believes, hopes, loves, one who bears witness to God's forgiving and deifying grace through his word and particularly through his life, who is cheerful and unruffled, then we have said something very generally Christian and yet something about the priesthood. Then such a priestly celebration, without betraying its nature, can itself become also an occasion of reflection on what it means to be a Christian and what it means indeed to each one of us.

Acceptance by each of his own mission

There was a time when the clergy in a people's Church held a special, privileged social position and power which existed independently of the faith, the brotherly love, and the loyalty of the laity, the members of the Church. That time seems to have come or to be rapidly coming to an end. In the future Church, which will be sustained only or almost only by the freely chosen faith of the individuals and by their fraternal desire for the Church, a Church in which the real effectiveness of office – without detriment to its origin from Christ and his mandate – is founded on the free adherence of all believers, there will be no place (beyond the unavoidable dissensions of a society with many distributed functions) for either anticlerical or antilaical feelings.

The priest will then be gratefully aware that he is called by God to serve his brothers by breaking for them the bread of life as preacher and as liturgical leader, by helping them to endure life, by accompanying them fraternally on the way of life right to the last station. But the layman will be grateful that God's grace led someone in the Church to take on an office which brings no earthly advantage but is a service. Thus all will be able to share in a 'priestly celebration', since it is one of the small feasts of the Church in which everyone, priest and layman, accepts his mission, and they will know as brothers that one helps the other and each does what is his to do.

THE FUTURE OF
RELIGIOUS ORDERS IN THE WORLD
AND CHURCH OF TODAY

The following text is based on a lecture given by the author in September 1970 to a large group of his fellow-Jesuits. Since the allusions to this community are very general, the lecture may be useful for all orders in the present situation.

The present situation

If we try to reduce the basic problem of Church and orders today and in the immediate future to a single and common formula, we might say that Church, statement of faith, worship, religious life, life in the orders, work in the orders, have also ceased to be obviously socially relevant at that point where *we ourselves* want to be identical, to live and work as identical, with ourselves. Faith, Church, and the idea of the religious life had always created in society – even in secular society – their objectification in words, in institutions, in something like life-styles, providing concrete ideals to be followed. This objectification was taken for granted in the secular society in which and in the light of which we live in fact as Christians, Catholics, and members of a religious order, even though in the wider environment of our sphere of existence at that time too other views of the world and interpretations of human life existed and were given objective social expression. *Within* our proper sphere of existence, presenting a symbiosis of sacred and secular, there were of course some things that were disputed, questioned, problematical. But the greater part of this ecclesial-secular sphere of existence belonging to ourselves was something taken for granted, without reflection, on which we lived unquestioningly. It was more or less the same as it is now in our country, where we men don't usually get excited about appearing in public in jacket and trousers, although it is not something absolutely to be taken for granted and although we older men in the order went about for long enough in cassocks.

Theoretically we knew indeed that this concrete sphere of existence, taken for granted in public life, required in its content and concrete form the *free* ratification of *faith* on our side and became personally authentic and significant for salvation only in this free obedience of faith, which itself had its very diverse forms and grades. But this sphere of existence was in fact obvious and ultimately undisputed. We older ones need only look back to our novitiate or the past decades of our life in the order to see how all this existed and was accepted as obvious and beyond discussion, just as we accept the fact that we have a head and two legs and that the weather alternates between sunshine and rain. We certainly put our whole personal and also critical mind and our heart too into this reality; but it was essentially obvious, simply given in advance and guaranteed by the very fact that the public character of this narrower sphere of existence of ours was taken for granted in such a way that our commitment to it made sense and that such a life was worth living.

All this held – of course, in the most varied forms and degrees – not only for the order, but for Christianity and the Church altogether, particularly from the eighteenth century and into the twentieth. During this time we were on the defensive, with a kind of ghetto-mentality, turned in upon ourselves in our political attitudes, with the result that the narrower sphere of existence in which and in the light of which we really lived maintained its homogeneousness and obviousness; whatever threatened it remained outside and was excluded *a priori* by a love–hate mentality as something alien, not to be taken seriously as worth integrating into our own life, no more than a medicine man would be considered worth consulting in our ailments.

Today everything is different: both in the Church and in the orders and for the same reasons. To put it crudely, there is nothing more that can be taken for granted in our own sphere of existence and there is nothing coming from outside which might not sooner or later enter into our own outlook on the world and our own way of life. The formerly separate ghetto-like spheres of existence standing alongside one another, almost like the denominationally uniform states of the seventeenth and eighteenth centuries, leading their separate lives, have merged into each other. We are no longer surprised by the fact that there are Protestants and atheists, that there are the most varied moral life-styles; each of us has become even inwardly the neighbour of everyone else, so that the other's mind and life have become a real possibility, an opportunity, and a temptation.

Today it is becoming increasingly impossible to accept and ratify our Christian and ecclesial life and our life in the order as something obviously given in advance, aware that this would remain a public and authentic reality even if we ourselves disavowed it; what we now have to do (again putting it, of course, somewhat crudely and in a very general way) is to realize and build up for ourselves what was formerly simply given in advance. The public realities of the Church and the orders are no longer supports, giving us the feeling of security and enabling us freely to shape our lives, but must themselves be supported by us: they are no longer the producers, but the products of our life's decision.

As we said, all this is expressed very generally. There are, of course, considerable differences between old and young, between the different intellectual and educational levels, between particular regions in our own country with greater or less relics of still unquestioned tradition, between particular countries in the Church, between the lower and higher clergy, and so on, and finally also between particular individuals in their disposition and their lot in life. But, while admitting these differences as obvious and even as very considerable, the above description of our present situation as it affects Christianity, Church, and orders remains correct.

The future situation

We shall not go into more detail here. We shall simply presuppose the above description as more or less correct and as understood. But in view of this we may expect this new situation of ours to remain by and large that of the immediate future. Of course, in addition to families and small groups sharing the same outlook on the world and upholding a common tradition, new circles are constantly emerging like islands within society as a whole, which have a meaning and a role for the individual similar to those of the former homogeneous social groups which we older people once took for granted and have had to abandon. Such new formations are certainly legitimate in themselves, since everyone attempting freely to shape his life needs to be relieved of some of his burdens by something already available, not needing to be specially formed but simply to be adopted. But this will not involve any substantial change for the individual in the basic situation of Christianity, Church, and orders. In this new situation, which is likely to persist for a long time, life will no longer be shaped by the weight of a pre-existing tradition but by the individual's free decision and its objective expressions. We shall have to face calmly the lasting consequences of these decisions, and they will have to be interpreted, at least up to a point, different from the apparently similar conditions arising from former basic situations.

When there is faith and personal ecclesial and religious life, it will be possible more easily than formerly to interpret such decisions as really personal, as faith in the theological and not merely social sense. But we shall have to accept without regret the fact that we can rely less than formerly on the individual in Church and order from the least to the greatest: for, to be exact, we were not relying at all in the past on the firmness and depth of an individual's personal decision, but really on the stability of the ideological conditions supporting that individual on whom we thought we could build as on a rock. For the same reasons personal decisions will constantly have to be made afresh and they will take longer to mature than used to be the case, since it was easier to be identified once and for all with the stable social institutionalisms and the undisputed dominant ideologies involved in the existence of Church and orders.

In future we shall no longer have any reason to be surprised when even older people are occasionally critical in regard to faith, life in a religious order, celibacy, and many other things which formerly – at least once they had been accepted and experienced for a time – sustained us and scarcely needed to be sustained themselves. In future we shall have no reason to be surprised that the life-styles of individuals, by the very fact that they are not given in *advance* as self-evident in the ecclesial and religious society, differ more than they used to do. In future there will inevitably be more spontaneity and creativity in the religious orders and in the Church, and indeed more frequently than formerly when everything was more in conformity with tradition and moved more slowly and changes took place mainly without reflection or planning. But for this reason there will also be more, and more violent, conflicts about policy within the orders, different styles of pastoral care, more pluralism in theology, than formerly. Authority in

Church and orders will no longer be something obviously to be accepted, which the individual can neither attack nor evade, but – to be really effective (which is not the same as having a legitimate moral claim) – will constantly have to be renewed by the free choice of individuals and constantly earned afresh by its holders.

This situation, with these pleasant and unpleasant consequences, must be presupposed as inevitable and lasting for the future. We must simply get used to this without fuss and stop moaning; we must recognize that the situation is one which is by no means opposed to Christianity and to the nature of a free personal faith, even though it is one which has not existed for a millennium and a half.

We must get used to it; but this also means in particular coming to recognize that we cannot escape this state of social insecurity simply by giving up Christianity, Church, and religious life. It seems to me that there were or still are too many people in the orders who think that by giving up their former Christian or religious life and accepting insecurity they would find clear, universally acknowledged, obvious reality. This is pure folly, itself the result of the old mentality which they think they are overcoming. Such people seem to me (prior to all deeper considerations) to be like those who sell shares during a slump, use the money to buy still worse shares, and then think that all is saved.

Of course higher authorities in the Church should also stop moaning and hoping that the old times will come back again. We should be cautious – and indeed in the light also of this new situation – in judging those who leave the order or the Church or both, but neither have we any reason to abandon in an undignified way our own self-understanding and act as if others had only done what we have not yet found the courage to do. And those who depart in this way should have found the courage for their action without having to be strengthened in it by our whole- or half-hearted approval.

The way of faith into an unknown future

Even though such a situation is foreseen as inescapable, the concrete future of Christianity, the Church, and the orders remains largely hidden from us. The profession of faith in Jesus Christ, crucified and risen, as the mediator of our salvation, and the Church will endure, and this very fact itself belongs to the hope of our faith in which we, challenged or not, have invested our whole existence. But what this means more exactly, what will be the historical and social appearance of the Church and of Catholic Christianity in the future, is largely hidden from us. The *docta ignorantia futuri* in this respect goes much further than we think or would welcome. But just to know and endure this is part of the situation of faith and of faith itself, and cannot surprise us.

In the last resort, we do not have to ask the futurologists for any prognoses for Church and orders and then regulate our life, our attitude to Church and order, in the light of this information. We have to fight for a victory without prognoses of this victory. Only to those who fight in this way is a promise given. Prognoses of a positive and, even more, of a negative character in these matters have been handed out for at least two and a half centuries, from the age of the Enlightenment. Neither the prophesying of the pious visionaries nor the forecasts of the rationalistic sceptics about the imminent decline of Christianity, Church, and papacy have hitherto been proved true. Christianity remained and remains *and* became quite different from what both friend and foe had conjectured.

We should not always want *a priori* to swim against the current at a particular time, as if simply by doing this we could guarantee to find the right direction in every case. But the opposite is just as false. Many who tried to jump on the train as it was moving fell under the wheels; or the train came to a stop after a short journey. Is Christianity understood as a profession of faith in the absolute incomprehensible mystery of our existence which embraces us, forgiving us and liberating us into its own infinity, and which we call God? Is it the profession of faith in Jesus Christ, whose lot continually brings home to us the closeness of this mystery as our absolute future? the profession of faith in the community of those who believe in this way and which is called Church, with an unbiased, sober attitude to its historicity which prevents us from taking refuge in abstract ideologies or, still more, from submitting to an evil tyranny of the present, of history and society? If this is where we stand, it is really impossible to see how anything could seriously theraten Christianity, apart from the scepticism of the rationalist who simply cannot any longer manage to find a meaning at all in the one totality of his existence. To put it quite plainly, do we want to be weary sceptics who conceal their despair from themselves, perhaps with the aid of a little humanism (incidentally, of a very respectable kind)? Or have we the courage to belong to those Christians of the future who neither abandon the historical heritage of ecclesial Christianity nor glorify it in a way that is no longer possible (as the clergy used to do), but stick to the incomprehensible meaning of their existence as it was brought home to us in Jesus of Nazareth and which is the living God himself? I think, therefore, that we can be content to live with the *docta ignorantia futuri* in regard to Christianity and the Church.

Obviously, the promise of the future of a religious order in the Church is not assured as faith in Jesus Christ is assured. But neither do we need, it seems to me, to prognosticate already the future of an order 200 years hence. This would be quite superfluous. We can be quite sure that in an enduring Church there will always be also a social, particular institutionalizing of the Christian life in certain radical forms, that in this sense therefore the religious life will exist also in the future. But, for the rest, we can live with the *docta ignorantia futuri* in regard to the life of the order as a concrete expression of our faith and hope, without indulging our curiosity in trying to anticipate the future.

We have sufficient reasons to carry out the life of our order today as something meaningful. But this presupposes that we wish to remain truly believing, determined Christians and accept realistically and unemotionally the fact that a change in our way of life might be a serious possibility only if we were convinced that we could not only realize in the abstract, but would also realize in fact concretely in this new way of life, more faith, hope, and love, more unselfish labour and service to man, more self-denial, or whatever we like to call it. I don't think it belongs to the resolute loyalty, to the vocation, of a religious to question the possibility of this sort of thing in *every* case. But I may be permitted to think that I have rarely, if ever, come across anything of the kind among those who leave the order. However this may be, each must decide for himself and the responsibility for the decision must be accepted individually and by each one for himself. The fact that many have departed and are still departing does not authorize someone else to do the same thing.

The necessity of experiments

Christianity, Church, and orders will not only have to live in a new situation, not only have to enter boldly and resolutely on a future which cannot be prognosticated, they will also have to make experiments. Since Vatican II there has been a lot of talk about experiments. It seems to me, however, that people understand 'experiment' in two ways: from *above*, inoffensive variations of thought-styles and life-styles which, however they turn out, make no significant changes and can be clearly seen from the start to be possible and unobjectionable; and often from *below*, purely arbitrary activities marked by prejudices which every honest and reasonable person, in the light of history and experience of life, can really easily recognize as such.

'Experiment' means neither of these things. I think that there can and must certainly be experiments which are not and cannot be *a priori* approved expressly and officially from above and which are nevertheless legitimate. If such experiments are to be distinguished from folly, immediately palpable prejudice, irresponsible caprice, then they must presuppose the existence and effectiveness of a responsibility *below* which cannot and need not always and in every case be sanctioned expressly by authority in Church and order to be legitimate, and yet which is the very opposite of arbitrariness and libertinism and is exercised with the utmost self-criticism and modesty.

There is a zone of life and action which cannot be expressly authorized by those who hold office, so far as the latter have to work with sovereign authority and not with personal mutual trust, in which nevertheless not everything is permitted merely because it is not officially forbidden. Of course there has always been this zone, but it was formerly comparatively narrow under conditions which were taken for granted and imposed a certain uniformity on everything, and for that reason it was scarely noticeable, did not become sufficiently an object of moral and practical reflection. We cannot again really institutionalize life within this zone and tie it to fixed norms of procedure. But we could certainly develop better than hitherto certain rules of the *game* and develop and strengthen the responsibility of all for experiments in the sense indicated.

Church and orders will in any case, now and in the future, have to experiment more, and we really cannot know in advance what will emerge from such experiments; an experiment can be necessary and legitimate even though it fails; institutions and individuals should have the courage to undertake such experiments, but also the courage coolly and expressly to admit that one of them has brought us into a blind alley, that we have to turn back, declare an experiment finished, without disavowing as stupid or immoral those who made it – who were supposed in fact to be self-critical – particularly since obstinate persistence in an existing tradition is also an experiment and very often a bad one from the start. An experiment within a particular society and therefore within the church or an order does not, at any rate for the most part, presuppose a properly official approval from above, although this does not mean that authority in a society is bound to tolerate any sort of experiment merely because it is not required to give a positive approbation. But experiments outside the strictly private life of an individual are certainly not possible if there has been no preliminary discussion and planning together.

This sort of necessary dialogue is indeed officially commended on all sides, high and low, in the Church as an ideal. But, it seems to me, there is not very much of it yet to be found. People still talk too often at cross-purposes; they are still inclined to regard the other person (not in theory of course, but certainly in practice) too easily as stupid, traditionalistic, revolutionary, wooden or immature, if he is not of the same opinion as themselves. True self-criticism is still rare. I have really very seldom met a superior or a subject who admitted he was wrong and had therefore changed his opinion. Self-criticism is still tacitly regarded as a kind of moral suicide, in the same way that no one will admit to a neurosis which cannot be overcome merely by a moral effort aided by a naïve spiritual director.

It is unpleasant to live at the experimental stage: the stage of uncertainties, of diversities of opinion, of possible conflicts of policy. But the situation is relieved by the knowledge that this sort of thing is unavoidable today and therefore normal. If, in the Church or in an order, people set to work in a proper spirit of self-criticism, if they avoid both in theory and practice prejudices which can really be quickly detected as such with the aid of self-criticism, if they avoid both in theory and practice prejudices which can really be quickly detected as such with the aid of self-criticism and good will, if the authorities in Church and order have the courage clearly and emphatically to reject certain experiments and the ability to win the support of reasonable people for their policy, then it will be possible in the last resort to live peacefully and fraternally together in such a situation, without those in authority thinking that they can issue a prohibition only if everything is forbidden from the start which they have not expressly permitted.

All this of course is very abstract. It is nevertheless important – and really no more than the expression in secular language of the theological truth that the Spirit can breathe in the Church without previously obtaining official permission – that authority may certainly test the spirits but not extinguish the Spirit, that those who are not office-holders are also responsible for peace, love, and even order in the Church, that their spirit must be tested by the fruits they produce and that the Spirit of Christ does not breathe where there is no unselfishness, modesty, or readiness for sacrifice.

Loyalty in the midst of change

I would like to try now to make just a couple of obvious remarks on our religious life in the future. I have already said that, in my opinion (which should not be taken as a criterion), we need not for the time being consider the future of the order a hundred years hence, since even the smartest futurologist of today can at most act as if he were planning so far in advance because he can perhaps correctly foresee some few moments of this future. We are talking therefore about *the* order, our order, and in the immediate future. Seen in this way, it has a reason for its existence and a task to perform. Anyone who does not understand this is arguing, it seems to me, on the basis of reflections on a future about which we can really know nothing.

We have today a meaning and a task; this task is not insignificant merely because it formerly perhaps had a greater importance and a more central place in the Church. We do not in fact choose for ourselves our life or times, the opportunities for our activity. If someone wanted to abandon our life's meaning and our task, he would first have to show that he knows and can realize a greater and in the long run more significant way of life. In almost fifty years of my life in the order I have come across not a few such attempts and fresh starts elsewhere. We need only recall the many secular institutes and other communities with the character of a religious order, which started out with the proud feeling that with them the new age was dawning and they had the keys to the doors of the future. It never really lasted long and they too fell under the law, which is in fact ours, of holding out in hope in a wintry time and having an understanding for the lonely greatness which lies in such an attitude of silent, uncomplaining loyalty.

It follows that all attempts to change the functions of this order must be rejected. We have to make experiments, have the courage to change ourselves, to see and seize on new tasks and to give up old ones, to march into a future unknown to us. But we have the right and duty to maintain the law under which we entered, even though distinguishing between the enduring Spirit and his constantly changing concrete manifestation is itself in many respects the task (by no means easy to accomplish) of the immediate future. But there are certain characteristics peculiar to our order which must remain and which, if they are resolutely lived out, contain also a promise for the future. These include the fact that we are an order of men in the Church, an institutional community for preaching the Gospel in the service of the Church; that, despite all new orientations which are constantly required here too, we are a community of life *and* work in one, and therefore not a secular institute in which these two factors may in principle be separated; that we are not a group of sympathetic individuals, but a community defined by service to the cause, in which what is finest in brotherly love is put unselfishly at the service of the cause – that is, of the *other* people.

No order, if it is rationally understood, can be or wants to be the field for realizing *all* that can be conceived of what is noble, human, and Christian together and at one stroke. To think otherwise or to strive to achieve all this would be childish and stupid. Every life has a definite shape and size only if it can renounce a great deal that is worth seeking for its own sake, in order to realize what properly belongs to it. Even allowing for this, our order still has sufficiently wide scope and can certainly discover more of its extent in one respect or another. But it must remain true to its spirit and innermost law: there is no reason why it should allow itself to be used for a new function by men who for some odd reason want to remain Jesuits and therefore want to turn the order into whatever suddenly strikes them as important and a source of perfect bliss in life and in the Church: a company of professional actors or perhaps a group of newly-weds. A bee-keeping association and a rabbit-breeding association are both thoroughly appropriate and desirable enterprises. But we ought not to want to turn one into the other. If that is the way we think, we should leave the association and seek its ideals elsewhere.

To make these obvious remarks, the truth of which has evidently not dawned on everybody today, is of course not to deny that there are *border-line* questions: whether an idea which happens to be new might nevertheless be adopted as in conformity with the spirit of the order and as the precept of the day. But, despite all these recognized marginal uncertainties, there are also frontiers which are and should remain quite clear. Hence, in my opinion, it would be conceivable by way of experiment for different houses of our order to develop different mentalities corresponding to their very diverse tasks and even to institutionalize these up to a point and give them a certain permanence. But we neither need nor want separate provinces in our order in the style of the reformed provinces of the older orders in the fifteenth and sixteenth centuries, although recently a few of our colleagues in Spain evidently thought they might be able in this way to save the old spirit in the face of some new corruptions of the spirit.

The three vows

These marginal remarks should include something about the three vows. As far as *poverty* is concerned, it seems clear to everybody that the aspect of our life-style described by this term must be freshly thought out. The question is whether in our order this ideal must be orientated more to sharing the lot of those who are really down and out socially and economically, or (assuming of course that our life-style is modest and critical of the consumer society) to the requirements of a common life through which each of us belongs to a community which is also economically a unity. I think that, in view of our other tasks, we may and should decide dispassionately and modestly for the second alternative now and also for the future. The other alternative is certainly a great ideal which should always stir us out of our complacency; in certain countries and in certain circumstances it might be something required of us also on the basis of our other conception of poverty. All the same, I think we should have the courage to be ourselves and not Charles de Foucauld's Little Brothers of Jesus.

Essentially we human beings are striving, with some prospect of success and in a society which is being dynamically transformed, for an economic situation in which there will no longer be starving, socially degraded people at all. To want to imitate in our own life-style that of the down-and-outs would be foolish and would make an emergency economic situation an ideal in itself. The conception of poverty which I regard as right for us has therefore the greater chance for the *future*. I know of course that particular, practical questions are not solved by this general orientation. It is also clear to me that what is really meant – for this orientation certainly has a meaning, even a spiritual meaning – would perhaps better not be called 'poverty' at all; in this way we could avoid many misunderstandings among people outside and also much superfluous moral theological casuistry among ourselves.

In regard to *renunciation of marriage* for religious motives, it must first of all be said that the fundamental meaning of this renunciation is guaranteed by the Gospel and can be genuinely realized even today. How many today and in the future are called to it is a theoretical question: the individual in practice must and can quite firmly make his life's decision without regard to what others may be doing. We should not be too quick to turn the theology of this life's vocation into a high-flown mythology. There are even secular tasks which at least in particular, concrete cases have imposed celibacy or made marriage inadvisable without the person involved necessarily breaking down in the situation or feeling frustrated at the deepest level.

I think we should first of all see our celibacy in this way, realistically and dispassionately, in the light of everyday life. Then, anyway in a humanly legitimate and Christian life, a point will constantly be reached at which such a renunciation can be rightly mastered and endured only be being achieved as part of that free choice with which a person by his own efforts approaches – at the latest in death – the renunciation in which he loses everything:

he is forced to decide whether he can see this radical deprivation as participation in the death of Jesus.

Life and all the motivation of life in the concrete is very complex and therefore so is the motivation for celibacy. We need not be surprised then if a theologically reflex analysis of this motivation only brings to light some parts of it, which in themselves are not entirely convincing: we are thus thrown back on the complex unity of this motivation in the whole length and breadth of our life, which must be experienced if it is to be understood.

In principle, the problematic of the celibacy of the secular priest is not our concern. Psychologically it may be the case that we entered a religious order requiring celibacy because we wanted to become and have become priests, who are bound by celibacy whether in an order or not. But, in the light of the meaning and nature of our vocation, we ought gradually have come to see celibacy as part of our religious life as such. For the rest, at a time when exclusive, monogamous enduring marriage has become questionable for many people, not as a result merely of libertinism, but also for reasons which are not without objective weight even though ultimately wrong, we should not act as if marriage provided a solution to all human problems, forgetting that marriage too is subject to the law which we call in a somewhat old-fashioned terminology the 'cross of Christ'.

As far as *obedience* in the order is concerned, we should first of all observe coolly and self-critically that there are certainly few callings where there is as much freedom as with us. Furthermore we should distinguish between the question of what a superior can legitimately order and the question of how far and with what motivation a subject must obey when he is given an order properly so-called. As far as the first question is concerned, it must be stated forthrightly that with us the superior's order must be oriented purely and simply to its objective expediency and nothing else. Service to man and, of course, the interest properly understood of the subject are the sole criteria by which the legitimacy of an order must be judged, so far as the order has still to be given and must be given by the superior in the light of his responsibility.

As far as the second question is concerned, it must be said first of all that it is always part of the subject's duty in conscience to judge the moral legitimacy of a given order, that, even with the best will in the world on the part of the superior, a particular order may be not only in some way irrelevant and inexpedient, but so much so that it must be described as immoral and the subject must refuse to carry it out. But it must be recognized also that different opinions may persist about the expediency of some orders, although it is impossible to describe any of the latter as essentially immoral. The other tacit assumption that any order which is less relevant or not as good as it might be in human terms is *ipso facto* immoral is the result of an unworldly illusionism and a failure to appreciate the obscurity and ambivalence of many human realities. If someone thinks that an order regarded objectively is not entirely right, but cannot, if he is honestly self-critical and modest, reject it as immoral, he must obey it without fuss, resolutely, and realistically. Life everywhere requires this, as also does work undertaken as a common task, which is quite impossible without a structured collaboration.

This very unmythological substantiation of obedience is sufficient in itself at least superficially, particularly since there is no great danger today of superiors really intruding upon that sphere which truly and properly remains private to the individual alone, even in the order and even though formerly indiscreet intrusions beyond these limits were by no means rare. This is not to dispute the fact that a forthright demand for obedience for the sake of the functioning of a working community may in the concrete impose extreme and cruel sacrifices on individuals. We should not plaintively and self-pityingly act as if such cases often occurred in the life of a particular order. This is simply not true with regard to normal people who are ready to make demands on themselves. Such cases can occur, but in the last resort there is nothing really particularly odd about them.

Essentially, nothing more is required here than what can really be demanded sometime and somewhere from any human being: the acceptance in grace of a greater or smaller part of the incomprehensibility of existence, achieved as a sharing in the lot of Jesus. The fact that this incomprehensibility is imposed on a person sometimes without any contribution of his own, at other times while presupposing his own decisions or fidelity to these, makes no essential difference, particularly since the demarcations between the two cases are very fluid. If such obedience makes sense in itself, if we are approaching – and some are gloating over the possibility – an age of greater human socializing, if unselfish

service particularly tomorrow will be the sole real form of freedom, then there seems to be no reason why in the future there
could be no order in which obedience counts among its life's
ideals.

Social commitment or more

There is one final observation to be made. It seems that many
younger men among us feel that social commitment in the struggle
for the freedom and rights of men (to express it cautiously) is *the*
experience of life from which, if at all, they can best gain an
understanding of the life of the order. The question then is only
whether they find this horizontalism of supreme importance as an
approach to understanding the religious life and as an indispensable dimension of their life in the order, or whether they want
to reduce our religious life completely to an exclusive horizontalism.
The first is legitimate, the second must be radically rejected. The
casuistry which exists or occurs to us in this respect for questions
concerning the concrete shape of life in the order in the future
cannot be discussed here. In principle, it is possible for us to find
by experimenting new forms for such a social commitment, which
are not only compatible with our religious life but positively
required in the future by the nature of an apostolic order. But
even then we are religious and Jesuits only if all this originates
in an explicitly grasped relationship to God and in the Church's
mission of salvation as such. For even then we have to be something
more than and different from people radically committed to justice
and peace in the world. This other 'more' does not then divide
our heart, but only makes this social commitment more radical.

There is, however, still something to be said about what is thus
admitted without prejudice and even recommended. As Jesuits and
priests, particularly for tomorrow, we ought to have a new and
original attitude – corresponding to the historical and social situation of tomorrow and not of yesterday – to what people called
and still call by an old and somewhat threadbare word 'spirituality'.
It is simply not true, but really a very old-fashioned and marginal
illusion, to think that the people of tomorrow would expect of us
nothing but social commitment, secular humanism, and fraternity.
If we talk to people behind the Iron Curtain – people living under
a socialism which for many of us, despite our reservations and
allowance for exaggeration, is still something of an ideal – we

observe that they expect from us a straight answer to those ultimate questions which are not answered by any socialism or by any earthly paradise whether socialist or capitalist in character. But if the consumer society has made us superficial, if we ourselves have not had any original experience of God, if we have not made an effort to let others share in an initiation into such an experience of God, then of course all that is left to us is to take refuge in a secular horizontalism which thus attempts to interpret and to live in an exclusively horizontal fashion the life of our own order. But this sort of thing is not only objectively false, but really old-fashioned: an attempt to keep up with something which is already becoming old-fashioned and was new before we came across it.

Shall we never succeed then in foreseeing and bringing on what is really new and coming? But this new and coming reality – for all the valid social commitment on which we badly need to catch up – is the spiritual, the experience of God, the taste of eternity, solid assurance in all the absurdity of existence which no social development can spirit away, which precisely then seizes the individual still more terrifyingly in his solitude. Why have we so few who are wise, so few who pray, who by their abandonment to God just do *not* create the impression of being old-fashioned, so few retreat-directors who can help the individual in the ultimate decisions of his life without naïve presumption?

Why do we think that spirituality in a genuine, radical sense is an old-fashioned affair, although we are in fact living at a time when those who are really young are even liable to run away from the banal desolation of a rationalized and technicized age, even with the aid of drugs if there is no other way out? Why do we try in the last resort to keep the average petty bourgeois with us with the aid of commonplace slogans and ideals and do not succeed in saying the liberating word of salvation to the lonely, to those who are enduring the radical dubiousness of our existence without false analgesics, to the few who are really important? This somewhat hidebound commonplace spirituality as it existed before the First World War in the orders, even with us, at least in outward behaviour, and which had too great an influence on the religious life, may belong to the past and young people may rightly say that it means nothing to them. Nevertheless, there is a true future for a new, original spirituality in the order and in the Church.

'MAKING SACRIFICES'
OR EVERYDAY RENUNCIATION

It has become customary today to criticize the spirituality, the style of the spiritual life of nuns of former generations. But we must not be too hasty in our criticism and we might well wonder if we ourselves, with our modern life-style, have brought into the world more love, more unselfish service to our neighbours, more love of God than former generations of religious orders.

Certainly some of this criticism is justified. Not a little of what once was good is no longer so, simply because the situation in which we live has changed. Among those things which should be critically considered in the spiritual ménage of the nun of former times is included the practice of 'making sacrifices'. People chose freely from time to time to impose on themselves some small renunciation from the most diverse fields of human life: they often made a collection of these sacrifices, 'offered' them for others, shared them occasionally with others in the form of a 'spiritual bouquet'; they called (this must be particularly emphasized) such practices 'sacrifices' and thus brought them into a misleading proximity to that which alone can properly be called sacrifice: the cross of Christ and the real imitation of the Crucified.

Such ascetic practices will perhaps strike most of us as so strange that it would seem pointless to talk about them at all. But it isn't as simple as that. There will still be many nuns who practise this sort of thing and many who do not perhaps take far too simple a view of the matter. What then are we to say here?

First of all, even today we must accept the fact that a genuine Christian life, real spirituality (or whatever name you give to what is meant here), cannot or can scarcely flourish without some organized exercise, without a form of training, without carrying out certain deliberately imposed tasks. If this is regarded as obvious for the artist, for the professional athlete, it cannot be considered wrong in the Christian life simply because this life has quite different dimensions from those of such secular callings. If the whole of man's life, and not merely certain 'areas', has to be integrated into the Christian life, then the latter – if it is to exist at all – must include at least up to a point and at the different phases of human development some training in particular modes of human behaviour.

A training of this kind (in attentiveness to the needs of others, in punctuality, in politeness, in discretion, and so on, not necessarily in this order of importance), in some sense deliberately undertaken, certainly does not as such touch the great, decisive moments of human life, nor can it replace these. We cannot summon or manipulate the great turning points of a radical faith, of a whole-hearted love for God, of a silently self-squandering love for a neighbour, of a hope against all hope. They are in a proper sense God's grace, coming as a surprise in their concrete shape even when we have tried to prepare for them; by God's sovereign providence they can be granted to someone who did not expect them or prepare for them.

The impossibility, however, of compelling the appearance of such moments of destiny, in which man is really able to surrender himself to God, does not mean that he has no need to prepare himself and adapt himself as he awaits them. The training of which we were speaking is the gesture of hopeful faith in the grace of God and, no matter how much it remains our own arduous deed, in itself and in regard to the real moments of God's grace it is once again grace. The exercises of the artist do not lose their value because they cannot compel creative inspiration. The artist who no longer exercises cannot complain if his creative intuition soon begins to fail or if he is no longer capable of turning this into a real work of art.

This training therefore, which we used to call 'making sacrifices' or somewhat disparagingly 'little sacrifices', ought to be orientated to those proper and radical achievements of the Christian life. This means that training may not be simply an activity running alongside the Christian life as such and an addition to it, what is known as a work of supererogation. The forms of renunciation required by life itself, if they are seen clearly and accepted deliberately, mean for the moment very much the same as what used to be called 'making sacrifices'. The Christian life requires us, for example, not to make unnecessary noise which disturbs others. If we do this with a certain persistence, shaking ourselves out of our inertia, then it is admittedly not a turning point of our Christian existence; but the other person in any case gets what we owe him independently of any 'loving disposition' of ours, and, above all, we are practising as far as this is possible for those moments of grace in which God will give us the power to love himself and our neighbour, without further regard for ourselves.

This is only a small example. We must find out for ourselves what our own life offers and demands in this respect by way of such 'training'. This is not to recommend a secular utilitarianism, but only to indicate the area in which to seek those small, everyday forms of renunciation which are important in the spiritual life even today. And if renunciation in these forms has been a little demythologized, no harm is done. For even in ordinary life they can be produced in the right way only if the spiritual man, in all his 'training', at the same time forgets himself once again and looks to God and his neighbour.

7
Pilgrim Church

TRUST WITHIN THE CHURCH

I would like to put before you a few modest reflections on trust within the Church. We are not talking about trusting the Church. To do so would involve a very great danger of ideologically hypostasizing the Church: it would not mean trusting any concrete individual and therefore it would be easy and would not hurt any of us. What I mean is trust *within* the Church, trust given to concrete human beings in the Church. Lay theologians[1] too – if their study of theology has been more than a sublime scholarly-theoretical curiosity – in the course of their life will enter into the Church's mission in some shape or form, will have to do with the Church, that is, with concrete individuals in the Church and particularly with those who hold office.

That is why our trust is called for. Not merely that, but among many other things of course: faith, courage, honesty, firmness of character, willingness to serve, and many other things which must govern relations between human beings if these relations are to be truly human and Christian. But, as we said, trust too, trust in those with whom we co-operate in the service of the Church's mission, trust also in the office-holders, although of course this is not to deny that the lay-theologian in the exercise of his mission also shares in the one office in the Church.

What is meant by trust? I don't want to give a definition drawn from philosophical or theological ethics. But I think that trust has to do with granting someone else a prior claim on our own life and action: we open ourselves out to the other person and up to a point place ourselves at his disposal, without being absolutely sure of the trustworthiness of the other. Trust means surrendering oneself to another without an ultimate reinsurance. If we are already absolutely certain that the other person is reliable, does not disappoint us, does not overtax us, does not demand more than he is permitted to demand, does not exploit us, pays back what he has been given, gives as much as he has received, we are not trusting the other, we are not entrusting ourselves to him, but (if we may put it in this way) we are trusting in our own knowledge of the other, we are not relying on the other, but on ourselves.

In trust we venture out to the other, forsake ourselves and our own security, and advance towards the other. Trust always means trusting an advance without security; it is essentially the risk of being disappointed, exploited, and of having our own uprightness turned (intentionally or unintentionally) into a weapon against ourselves. The situation is the same as that of love: this trust is a form of love. In both cases it is a question not of a deal, of give and take, not of a shrewd compromise between two egoisms, not of a calculation which we already know to be correct, but of the risk of having to give more than we receive, of knowing that what we give freely will be coolly taken for granted, of faith in the victory of truth and goodness even though this seems to be refuted a thousand times in life, of hope that love's Utopia is the true future which is really coming, of love which succeeds in achieving the improbable, of getting a person away from himself. Trust is the gift of ourselves in advance, in the venture of believing and hoping, without previous cover.

I will not dwell on the fact that people cannot live in close contact with one another without this trust, that it is something without which a person is not a Christian. To make this clear would in fact be the most important thing to be said about trust. But it would take too long.

I would rather give a more concrete explanation of the way in which trust means giving the other person a start. I don't think I need in this respect to make especially explicit every time the 'application' to people who co-operate with us in our service in the Church's mission or who hold office.

This trust as given in advance means first of all quite simply that we approach the other person taking it ultimately for granted that he cannot *a priori* be considered as more stupid or less upright and straightforward than we consider ourselves to be, as intelligent and upright people. Theoretically this is simply obvious. In practice however it is cruelly hard, if only because in the individual case we do find in fact that the other is at least more stupid; nor is this always an illusion. It is cruelly hard particularly since we are much more egoistic, more full of our own importance, more self-confident than we are able or willing to admit. If our opinion is charged with the whole weight of our feeling as individuals and if the other person does not agree with us or even makes a demand on us in the light of this opinion, it really is difficult not to regard him as stupid or malicious.

Recently I was deeply shocked to read in a newspaper, *Die Zeit*, how a former priest had charged the Pope with bad faith, simply because he did not agree with the encyclical on celibacy. Mostly we don't make it so clear. But often enough we act in a similar way. Where an opinion touches ourselves in our own existence, we consider our own alone to be true and the opposite explicable only as the result of stupidity or malice. And if we look for reasons for our own opinion, we can easily find a thousand. As soon as we consider the arguments on the other side, the slightest emotional load is enough to blow the fuse in our head.

This trust of the other person in the Church, if it is really given in advance, therefore implies self-criticism. In Mao Tse-tung's catechism self-criticism is one of the most important catchwords. Criticism in the Church today is written in large letters. Not entirely without reasons. But in the catechism of our heart the word 'self-criticism' should be written larger than we write it. We really could not but be shocked if we were to ask ourselves whether we know as much against ourselves as we bring forward against others, whether we are as critical of ourselves as of others. For we are convinced (not expressly and formally, but in the way our egoism normally functions) that we are more intelligent and upright than others, and in fact from the very start. We are not self-critical.

It is, however, only when we have a naturally, completely un-neurotic, almost serene and obvious self-critical attitude towards ourselves, which we maintain without having to pride ourselves on it, that we cease to be egoists and become single-minded human beings and Christians. We gain a wonderful, serene freedom from ourselves when we no longer need to make ourselves the criterion of truth, when we can laugh at ourselves, when self-critical behaviour has become natural to us. My father, who lectured in a teachers' training college, once reproved a student for giving an answer which he was supposed to have given himself in a previous lecture. When the student therefore defended himself, my father said: 'You don't have to repeat all the nonsense that I've said.' Of course he had not said it, but neither was he self-assured. Many decades ago I had a professor who smiled at a student as he entered the lecture-hall and said: 'Don't yawn. I haven't said anything yet.' Self-critical freedom from oneself is necessary. It is because we – we Germans particularly – are not self-critical that we are so intolerant, so humourless, so pig-headed and fanatical. Self-criticism is the presupposition of being able to give our trust in advance to the other person, in the Church too, convinced that it is not so certain that we are right, that it is the other perhaps who is right.

Only a person who is willing to serve can give his trust in advance. We are bound to have our own convictions, our own ideas, our own plans. But we should keep them fluid, in a self-critical spirit; we should be more expansive in our convictions, ready to make distinctions, more patiently wise: which does not mean that we want nothing more, can no longer say 'No', that we forgive everything because we understand everything. This self-critical growth in our convictions and decisions, if it is to be achieved within the Church, presupposes the will to serve. We find ourselves only if we forget ourselves in the service of a cause: of the cause of men, which is greater than ourselves.

This shifting of the Archimedean point away from ourselves, without which we never really rise above ourselves in order truly to find ourselves, is possible only if there is a real source of authority in our life really pressing us, which we have not manipulated in advance in the light of our own taste and judgement, to which we have conceded the disposal of ourselves. Otherwise we just fluctuate within the circle of our own subjective whims. We must serve something else in order to become free, something greater, to which we have conceded freely but really a true power of determination over ourselves.

We must be willing to serve, we must be willing to receive orders which have not already been refashioned simply by the subjectivity of our own private sphere. Only if we succeed in this do we become free from the most deeply hidden self-alienation: that which confuses the most subjectivistic ego with the true ego which is attained only by conquering ourselves, ultimately by reaching God, not merely by a cheap ideologizing of our own subjectivity but by really exposing ourselves to another, by serving. It is by being willing to do this that we give our trust in advance. For this trust implies a willingness to listen without having completely examined already what is being said.

Someone who gives his trust in advance will often be disappointed. He will not rarely find that his trust remains unrewarded, is perhaps exploited, taken for granted, and wasted. Often he will not know (and in the last resort there is no formal prescription for this) how he can unite what is precisely his own responsibility and his own firm conviction with self-critical scepticism towards his own opinion and with the will for service without reservation, how he can be trusting without being gullible or naïve. He will constantly be faced with the apparently insoluble task which was also faced by Jesus, of whom it was said that he trusted himself to no one, because he knew what was in man, and who in summing up his life said that he was giving himself up to men and for men unto death. But none of this means that trust is not possible in the Church, but only that this trust too is a miracle of God's grace, the folly of the cross, the Christian's self-denial, the imitation of the Crucified, the faith that unarmed, foolish-seeming love will be victorious.

How often within the Church do our tensions and conflicts move on a level which is infra-Christian. On both sides of course. But this does not dispense us from the Christian's task of finding for himself the Christian level, even though perhaps the other side will not accept it; it does not dispense us from beginning with ourselves, from trusting in advance and hoping against hope, from believing that we can really conquer evil by good. Trust is also part of this good.

TRANSLATOR'S NOTE

1 *Laientheologen* can mean both lay persons who are students of theology and lay-teachers of theology. Rahner is here addressing · students at the university of Münster.

THE DUTY OF DISCUSSION

A PLEA FOR CARDINAL SUENENS

Preliminary historical remarks

Leo Joseph Cardinal Suenens, Archbishop of Malines-Brussels and Primate of Belgium, gave an interview to Henri Fesquet which was published in *Le Monde*, 12 May 1970. Twelve months earlier the Cardinal had published in *Les Informations Catholiques Internationales* an interview which created a great stir at the time (I explained my reaction in *Publik* No. 27/69). Suenens, who had been one of those presiding at the Second Vatican Council, now in the post-conciliar period continues in this new interview the statement on urgent problems of the Church which he began in the earlier interview.

The new interview links up with the communiqué of the Dutch episcopate, declaring the desirability of admitting married priests in the Church in Holland and demanding a free discussion on the legislation on celibacy in the whole Church. Cardinal Suenens knows and says expressly that Paul VI several times rejected the opinion and wishes of the Dutch bishops, even after their communiqué. Nevertheless, for reasons of which more will be said later, Suenens continues this dialogue. He explains his reaction as his personal opinion and thus does not want to involve the Belgian episcopate as a whole. He expressly and intentionally avoids entering into the objective question of the Church's legislation as such on celibacy: he does not react to this either positively or negatively.

The theme of his interview is prior to this objective question: it is concerned with the question whether, in spite of Rome's 'No', there may and must be further discussion on this issue and who are the right people to take part in it. Suenens demands a dialogue on the question between pope and bishops, between bishops among themselves, between the individual bishops' conferences and particularly (this is perhaps the new aspect) between the individual bishop and his priests and the people of God in his diocese, so that on this account too he has more than a purely legal authorization for dialogue within the circle of those who hold office in the Church.

In handling these themes it was inevitable that Suenens should touch also on the more general question of appropriate form of Church government today. The timing of this interview was conditioned by the fact that a commission was then meeting in Rome to prepare for the next synod of bishops: Suenens' recommendations were therefore addressed particularly to that quarter. In an address on 15 May 1970 Paul VI (without expressly naming the cardinal) declared his 'painful astonishment' at the interview. He insisted that he was sticking unswervingly to the principles of the Second Vatican Council about collegiality in the Church, but that he would not let himself be tied down to a particular theological interpretation of this teaching.

The priests' councils (Flemish and Walloon) of the Cardinal's diocese in two declarations placed themselves unequivocally behind their bishop. Suenens himself went into the whole affair again in his sermon in Malines on Whit Sunday, on the occasion of the Pope's celebration of his golden priestly jubilee. He tried to make clear in this sermon why he had given the interview. He understood it as an act of fulfilment of his episcopal duty, as a public and frank expression of opinion, which is normal and salutary also in the Church and does not imply any lack of respect. His statement did not contain any depreciation of celibacy as such, which, he said, remains binding in any case on priests already ordained. He was only asking for the legal connection between priesthood and celibacy to be debated afresh. He wanted the Pope's declaration against further discussion of the celibacy question (*Osservatore Romano* 2/3 February 1970) to be reconsidered and the question then to be calmly and objectively discussed with the aid of experts in the priests' and pastoral councils. Suenens insisted that he did not want by these recommendations to prejudge any particular solution of the celibacy question. The further history of this interview cannot be recorded here.

What is a bishop to do?

In his interview Suenens describes very clearly the dilemma facing a bishop today. He looks at empty seminaries, he knows that an ever-increasing number of priests are leaving the ministry (in the past two years, says Suenens, in Holland alone 400 priests have left; in the U.S.A. there are far more); a bishop knows that his clergy are discussing in speech and writing the celibacy question in a way and to an extent that it was never discussed before. On the other hand, further discussion of this question is rejected.

What then is a bishop to do? Many young people in the Church with their present mentality can certainly quickly find an answer to this question, almost before it is formulated. But a bishop knows that he is in principle bound by the teaching of the first and second Vatican Councils, according to which the Pope possesses a universal and ordinary jurisdiction over all churches and also over all bishops; a bishop feels a bond of personal loyalty to the Pope. Nor can he take lightly the question whether express permission to continue the discussion would not psychologically and practically anticipate a negative reaction to the present legislation on celibacy. A bishop will also wonder if the continued discussion of the question may not also create a precedent for the treatment of other questions which in the concrete cannot or can scarcely be solved in practice in the same way. A bishop sees the implications of this problem for the theory and practice of the Church's government in general and thus knows that the Pope's appeal to his fundamental authority in this question cannot be set aside as it might seem to a number of people in the Church today.

On the other hand, the bishop is faced by the fact that he cannot ignore, that the discussion continues in the Church despite the Pope's protest. The bishop must admit that the cause of celibacy would be served least of all if he were to act as if this discussion did not exist, if he kept out of it simply by maintaining silence or by protesting together with the Pope. The bishop will admit that, according to the Catholic conception of episcopal office, he cannot consider himself merely as the recipient of orders from the Pope, but as ruling his diocese in the name of Christ and not of the Pope, and thus he has and must develop a responsibility and initiative of his own which he simply cannot shift off on to the Pope. He can then certainly not simply decide that he really has nothing to do but stand by the Pope's prohibition.

What, for instance, is the Archbishop of Belem in Brazil to do, in a diocese with more than 600,000 Catholics but with no candidates for the priesthood in his seminary for fifteen years and with ever-diminishing prospects of getting priests from abroad? Must he be *a priori* sure that what was going on among priests and people cannot be inspired by the Spirit of God? If he merely looks on without doing anything about further developments, must he not wonder whether he is not responsible for the way in which such movements develop in the Church? Must he not reflect on how he expects to influence such a movement at all if he refuses from the start to talk with those who sustain it? Must he not consider whether 'disobedience' below does not throw light on faults above? May he assume that he is involved in a conflict of duties (which, even according to traditional theology, could always be solved in principle), but that with limited time and limited oportunities of clarification he simply cannot reach a solution which is theoretically clear and approved by all simultaneously? May he perhaps admit that a passive attitude, although the least striking and so perhaps meeting with the least opposition, would for this very reason be certainly far from being the right solution?

Faced with this dilemma, Suenens decided to speak and not to be silent. He was evidently convinced that he could satisfy his duty as a bishop only in this way and so too did what really corresponds to the relationship rightly understood of a bishop to the Pope in the concrete situation. He evidently thought that misgivings and criticisms can be brought forward against a Pope's concrete decisions (church history books are certainly full of them) and not merely in regard to deceased popes or – in conversation among the electors when the Roman See is vacant – about a future pope. He will hold that there are in fact (as in human life, so too in the Church) particular situations of conflict which cannot be resolved completely simply by abstract principles alone or at least (you might say) can be resolved only by explicitly recognizing the abstract principle that there are cases of conflict which cannot be adequately mastered by the theoretically relevant principles alone.

Suenens will hold – and who could contradict him in principle and for all cases? – that occasionally true obedience might consist in infringing the letter of a law or of an order. He will certainly not let himself be frightened off this opinion by the lamentable fact that many thoughtless and fundamentally disobedient people will appeal to this principle, correct in itself but wrongly applied by them, in concrete cases, to the detriment of the Church. He will console himself with the thought that there are cases in which someone to the best of his knowledge and in all conscience must work out a decision which he cannot deduce for others in complete logical clarity from a number of general principles. He will hope that a pope too can understand, appreciate and tolerate such a decision within the unity and final peace of the Church, even though he himself to the best of his knowledge and in all conscience cannot agree with its content.

The theology of dialogue

We shall not discuss again the moral-theological question of the legitimacy of conduct contrary to the letter of the law or of a higher authority. But we may put forward some theological reflections on the dialogue recommended by Suenens and, on one particular issue, refused by the Pope. For his recommendation of a dialogue on the question of celibacy between pope and episcocate, between bishops and bishops' conferences among themselves, between bishops and priests and the faith, Suenens appeals to the principle of collegiality proclaimed more clearly than formerly at the Second Vatican Council. The Pope declares that this demand arises from a very particular theological interpretation of this Vatican teaching, an interpretation which he is not bound to share, and his refusal does not infringe the principle of collegiality.

Now in interpreting the Second Vatican Council on collegiality between pope and bishops there are undoubtedly real and possible differences of opinion on how a more subtle ecclesiology would have to reconcile the primacy of the pope – who is not merely *primus inter pares* of the episcopal college – with the doctrine of the supreme and plenary authority in the Church of the episcopate as a whole (with and under the pope). We may wonder whether the pope, even when he makes use of his primatial power outside a properly collegial act of the episcopate as a whole, nevertheless acts as head of the whole episcopate and, if so, whether certain consequences result also for the concrete form of such an act, or whether this is not the case at all. We may wonder what more concrete consequences (which are also in principle legally conceivable) result from the dogmatically indisputable fact that the pope cannot in principle abolish the whole episcopate as supreme bearer of authority in the Church and, for this very reason, cannot suppress in everything and forever the activity of this supreme subject of such authority.

What concrete conclusions thus emerge may be very contentious in the individual case, may in particular be themselves the object of papal decisions and as such remain in advance a *quaestio disputata* for theologians and canonists who discuss and dispute the opportuneness or inopportuneness of such possible activation of this supreme authority of the episcopate (for example, convening a general council, shaping the Roman synod of bishops so that it can be regarded as legally equivalent to a council). It is obvious that in ecclesiology and canon law there are open questions about the consequences of this teaching on the episcopate for the collegiate co-operation of pope and bishops in the normal life of the Church in *those* cases in which there is no question of a strictly collegial act of the whole episcopate, but of co-operation between episcopate and pope which is less clearly defined legally but nevertheless supremely important.

The fact that there must be such further co-operation is undisputed and is also expressly emphasized by Vatican II. As to *how* it can and should be organized in the concrete and in accordance with the circumstances, there can of course be differences of opinion. And the pope in such questions is certainly not bound to follow the particular opinion of a single group of bishops, theologians, and canonists. Of course, in this respect too, one thing should be clear and also undisputed, but in fact it is not: these concrete forms of collaboration between pope and episcopate should be largely laid down in concrete norms of canon law, which would be binding on pope and bishops (as pope and secular powers must keep to the terms of a concordat); they should not simply be thrown back from one case to another on the unforeseeable 'prudent judgement' of the pope alone.

Here perhaps is the sole, but practically very important point on which in our question there is not sufficient unanimity, although it should exist and could be established. It would in no way be an attack on or a curtailment of the papal primacy if the pope were to institutionalize to a large extent the exact form of that co-operation with the whole episcopate which is necessary today. Even if we were to interpret such a juridical institutionalization of the combined action of primate and episcopate, going beyond the little we have had hitherto, in terms analogous to those relating to concordats, with mutual recognition of 'privileges' (which would be welcomed by a very 'papally' minded canonist), what is really important today would still be possible. Pope and bishops would know exactly what their co-operation was about; it would no longer be possible for the pope to surprise bishops with important decisions which they could only note and on which they had not even been previously consulted.

Suenens' recommendation, however, of a bolder and more intensive dialogue between the authorities mentioned on important questions of life in the Church today – celibacy, for example – is by no means dependent on the different interpretations of the doctrine of collegiality. It is obvious even from statements of Vatican I and particularly from Vatican II that the pope, both in undertaking his teaching office and also in exercising his power to govern, must make use of suitable means (*media apta*) in order to be able on each occasion to reach the relevant decision. Such a decision is not always clear from the very beginning. In order to reach it, the pope does not receive any new revelations from above (as Vatican II expressly declares); the assistance of the Holy Spirit, which is promised him but does not operate with infallible certainty in every decision, may not be conceived mythologically as a perceptible 'inspiration' for himself alone, in the individual consciousness of the pope, but exists concretely precisely in the right use of the necessary means of human knowledge for reaching such a judgement.

If we are clear on this point, we can leave aside all the more subtle theological interpretation of collegiality in the Church and still come to the conclusion that Suenens' recommendation is justified. In such questions, where the concrete and also really effective solution depends on the actual social and psychological state of the Church – as it is and not as we would perhaps like it to be – how is the pope to know the concrete situation, to make use of the 'suitable means' for preparing his decision, except with the aid of intensive co-operation from the episcopate: that is, of open and frank dialogue? In the supremely complicated psychological and social situation of the world and the Church, the information required is quite different from that which sufficed in more patriarchal times when a benevolent father and prince with good will and his own estimate of what he had learned from particular cases knew more or less what he needed to know to make his decision. Today the flow of information upwards from below must be institutionalized and, through this institutionalization, care must be taken to see that what reaches the top is not merely casual information, and that information is not held up on the way if people don't want to know of it, or if it is opposed to the decision which people at the top are inclined to favour in the light of their personal experience of life, of their place-seeking or of their special theological viewpoint.

But how, for example, can such a necessary flow of information be adequately guaranteed if a Roman synod of bishops cannot even draw up an agenda for itself? How is it possible if bishops cannot themselves suggest a theme for dialogue with Rome, if they may not (as Suenens did) say that they want an open discussion on a particular topic? The episcopate is in any case today the indispensable and most easily activated co-ordinating centre for the information needed by the Roman Church leadership. Of course the episcopate is such only if it is itself engaged in a lively dialogue with priests and people, as Suenens insists.

If the dialogue between pope and episcopate as required by Suenens is so authorized in the light of that information which is among the 'suitable means', that is not to say of course that the provision of information is the sole justification of this dialogue or the one which touches its ultimate nature. The justification which reaches the essence of the dialogue within the Church must be based on a thoroughly worked out theology of fraternity and collegiality in the Church, of the Church as the one body of Christ, animated by the Spirit, driven in all its members by the Spirit, by the charisms which are not simply subject to the Church's ministry. But if the necessity of a dialogue results in the concrete from the simple need of information which is not manipulated, which is wide-ranging and accepted in its brutal harshness, if the dialogue cannot be arbitrarily brought to an end on the plea that no more could be learned from it than is already known, then Suenens' recommendation is obviously valid, independently of the question of its justification from the teaching of the Second Vatican Council or from a particular theological interpretation of that teaching.

On dialogue in the individual Churches

What is rather new in Cardinal Suenens' interview is really the demand for an intensification of dialogue in the individual churches, the national churches, and the dioceses, in the style of Holland and its pastoral synod. Suenens is convinced that a 'papalism' – by which is meant, not the dogma of Vatican I and its practical consequences, but a style of government which is time-conditioned, no longer appropriate and above all no longer effective today – must not be replaced by an 'episcopalism' which betrays the same defects on the plane of the individual churches as 'papalism' on the plane of the Church as a whole.

This of course does not mean that, from the standpoint of dogmatic theology or canon law, the relationship between bishop on the one side and priests and people on the other is or should be exactly the same as that which exists between pope and episcopate. But if Christ's promise and his Spirit are given in the first place to the Church as a whole, and for that reason to the Church's office in so far as it exercises within this whole a necessary function which does not belong in the same way to everyone in the Church, if a fraternity founded by the Spirit precedes all the justifiable differences of function on the part of the Church's members, if the Spirit gives charisms (which may seem very secular) to whom he wills, without regard to office and without always needing the intervention of the latter, then fraternal dialogue among all members of a particular church is really something to be taken for granted. It is in fact a duty arising from office itself, whose authority (by no means diminished in its real effectiveness, which is what properly counts) is largely dependent on the fact that it recognizes and fulfils itself this duty of dialogue.

On this plane too what has already been said about the necessity of a juridical institutionalization of this dialogue holds. It cannot be denied that such a dialogue is arduous, that it easily degenerates into a mere talking-shop, that it can even threaten positions which cannot be abandoned on matters of faith within the Church. But when, according to the normal teaching of the Church, it is a matter of human law and opinions which, despite their very practical consequences, are by no means ultimately binding, or when the ultimately binding character of a norm of faith or of law or of their interpretation is disputed, the bishops should enter into a frank dialogue with their priests and their people. Indeed, even within the Church, opinion polls can be appropriate if they genuinely reveal what the faithful are actually thinking, even though the actual existence of these opinions cannot *a priori* raise any claims to a plebiscite.

Over and above this, Suenens rightly insists that a bishop can really fully represent his own church in a bishops' conference or in a Roman synod only if he is really in living contact, in a continuous, frank dialogue with his priests and with his people. He may represent his diocese in virtue of canon law even without such a vital link with his church; but he would not represent his church fully – that is, humanly, in a spirit of Christian fraternity, charismatically – if he falls back on his isolated official competence and his solitary decisions which then too would remain unjustified in their isolation, if he surrounds himself with counsellors of his choice from whom he hears more or less from the start only what corresponds to his own outlook.

The Second Vatican Council says (*The Church in the Modern World*, No. 92):

> By virtue of her mission ... the Church stands forth as a sign of that brotherliness which allows honest dialogue and invigorates it. Such a mission requires in the first place that we have within the Church herself mutual esteem, reverence, and harmony, through the full recognition of lawful diversity. Thus all those who compose the open people of God, both pastors and the general faithful, can engage in dialogue with ever-abounding fruitfulness.

If we are really convinced that the Church can be the sign of fraternity for mankind as a whole only if she really succeeds in establishing a dialogue within her own boundaries, can it be so difficult to agree on the objects of such a dialogue? Can a dialogue be refused at the official level when it is anyway being carried on in the Church? Is Suenens' recommendation, made by a man conscious of his episcopal responsibility, unreasonable?

EXPERIMENT IN THE FIELD OF
CHRISTIANITY AND THE CHURCH

It is well known that many decrees of the Church (on liturgy, ecclesial-social structures, religious life, education, and so on) permit and recommend 'experiments'. But it seems that these recommendations fail to make clear what is meant by such 'experiments', if we take the term seriously, and what therefore is in fact recommended. Here are a few reflections on this question.

We must deny ourselves the indulgence (if we are not to lapse into vague talking) of reflecting on the history of ideas with reference to modern times as the age of (quantitative) experiment in the natural sciences and going on from there to its place in all exact sciences, or getting involved in a discussion of the nature of experiment in a strictly scientific sense. We might simply say that there can be no question here of this kind of scientific experiment. Man is a historical being and history as such is not really open to experiment in the form it takes in the natural sciences: there successful experiment enables us to make a certain and exact prognosis, which of course is quite impossible in history. In the human sphere as such, in history and therefore in the Church, if there is to be experiment at all, it must be in a sense which we still have to discover.

Experiment – transitory happening or permanent state?

We might perhaps find a way to deal with the problems raised here by asking first of all if the experiment of which we are thinking is a transitory happening, detached from its goal by a state of things in which no further experiment is necessary; or if this experiment is something like a continuous event which now belongs permanently to our way of life (in the world and in the Church), a 'permanent state'.

Mostly when we talk today about experiment in the life of the Church we tacitly assume that the first alternative is correct. We think that experiments cannot now be avoided, since the old style of life in the Church (which we experienced as stable and enduring) obviously no longer functions rightly; but the object of the experiment must be to reach another, a new state of things in the life of the Church, which however will be like the former in being clear, lasting, and stable. Evidently we are guided in this assumption by the example of experiments in natural science (at least as these are properly understood). The object of such experiments is to bring out a conclusion which then remains established and thus (at least in a certain sense, that is, when we are not reproducing an old experiment for the instruction of students) renders superfluous any further experiment in this matter.

But is this really a correct idea of the kind of experiment with which we are concerned here? We may doubt it. Of course we have no intention of disputing the fact that, even in the life of the Church in very many cases, or as an element in experiments, there are experiments which correspond to this model. Certainly in the field of liturgy or educational method, and so on, we can perform experiments which produce a definite result showing the suitability of a hitherto doubtful procedure (or prove the opposite as certain), so that a fixed (relatively unchangeable) procedure results for the (immediate) future. But is this experiment – which undoubtedly also exists and in very many cases – really the proper model, the basic model, of the kind of experiment which we feel to be necessary today in the Church? Is the situation perhaps different and in fact so very different that the word 'experiment' is only an utterly inadequate and easily misunderstood designation of what we really mean in this instance? This in fact does seem to be the case.

Experiment in natural science and in the Church

First of all, experiment within the Church has a relative value quite different from that of scientific experiment in 'nature'. An experiment in natural science does not itself change (at least not in practice) the nature on which it is supposed to provide information, or (if you want it otherwise) it is from the start an occurrence in nature equivalent to all other events or sequences of events. But experiment in the Church is an event within the Church herself, since there is no laboratory where experiments can take place, so to speak, alongside the Church. Even in the form of experiment the liturgy is really celebrated in a particular way, instruction is in fact given, other administrative practices are carried out. In fact an experiment in the Church is just not merely an experiment, but really a part of the Church's action and life. And the reservation that it has to cease if it doesn't work well does not alter the fact that the experiment results in the achievement of something seriously intended in the life of the Church which itself, in view of the one-way character of history, can never be retracted. Experiment in the Church has an existential character and can by no means be a game of sandcastles, a manoeuvre where only blank cartridges are used. The ethics of such experiments in the Church are partly determined by this fact.

There is another reason why experiment in the Church cannot be assimilated to a scientific experiment. The 'result' of the latter, even though not known in advance, is certain 'in itself' *before* the experiment and therefore presupposed. The result, as far as we can use this term at all, of an experiment in the Church as such and in the proper sense of the word (that is, as distinct from experiments in the broader sense or as in natural science, which, as we said, can and necessarily should exist *also* within the Church) is the effect of the experiment itself. It is an event arising from practical reason and freedom, not simply observed, accepted, confirmed by theoretical reason. This means that we experiment not merely to know what is, but in order to learn by experience what we *want*. We are looking for a decision, not a pre-existent fact, even though in this search for a decision the will is always formed also partly in the light of cognitive elements which go back to pre-existent facts.

With experiments in the Church it is ultimately a question not of discovering a know-how, of bringing out the best method, of how we can reach a goal fixed and unanimously accepted in advance, but of the experiment of freedom in which, as a result of a process of deliberation, a goal is chosen only by being devised. For the possible goals are not set out as already complete and known prior to a choice, so that we merely have to consider *which* in fact we want and what the means and methods suitable for its realization. It is a question rather of finding the goal itself, which we are still far from knowing exactly, of which we are only working out a preliminary outline.

Of course such creative outlines are also affected by existing facts and preconditions (particularly in the Church: in her self-understanding, in the already existing preliminary outline of her task, in her past experience, in the Gospel, in the situation which can be simply empirically observed to exist, and so on). But the new goal must be creatively outlined and cannot be deduced by a logical process from these preconditions and preconceptions; and (which is almost more important) the creation of such goals in turn modifies for man's knowledge and freedom these preconditions and preconceptions, both of man and the Church herself, with a kind of reverse effect (if we may express it in this way). A person's capacity is changed by the very act performed in virtue of that capacity.

Thus the goal of the experiment in a quite definite and radical sense is open and still unknown, despite all pre-existent 'essences' and knowledge of essences, as ground and horizon of all creative freedom. Experiment rightly understood brings surprises against which we are not insured by the knowledge and the obligation of the norms in the light of which we experiment. Experiment is therefore properly speaking autonomous and bound only by the laws which it sets up itself and thus affirms in the very process of being carried out.

Church history as the radical experiment

In this sense we have always 'experimented' in history. For history, with its unceasing change, is itself the great experiment in which man's freedom is exercised, seeks new shores and a still unknown future. And the history of the Church in particular is such an experiment. For this history is the pilgrimage into the infinite incomprehensibility of God, which comes to an end only where there are no longer any roads or any frontiers. This history is the history of hope, to which the future is more important than the past, even though this future is hidden in the mystery of God; the history of hope, whose 'goal' (in the last resort) just cannot be planned, since it depends for its reality and its attainment on the inscrutable providence of God.

The starting point of this church history as pilgrimage into the unknown is certainly grasped in faith as firm and certain. But this starting point, which remains as the law of the way into God's remoteness from all ways, is the Crucified, who surrendered himself unconditionally into the hands of the Father in the experiment of his death and only so is accepted as the Risen one and gives us his Spirit, who breathes where he wills and not where we will. Church history is the most radical experiment: where it is not, where it becomes nervous traditionalism, it may perhaps still be the history of sinful man in the Church, but no longer of the Church as she ought to be according to the will of Jesus.

Planned history

What is or at least ought to be *new* in experiments in the Church today lies in the fact that we are *reflectively* aware of this experimental character of the Church's life and history: we are no longer merely enduring it, but we are expressly aware of it, try deliberately to foster it, actively and methodically strengthen it and thus attempt to speed it up. Experiment in the Church is the expressly cultivated, methodically promoted and accelerated part of *the* experiment which is necessarily involved in the history of the Church.

Experiment so understood within the experiment which is the Church is necessary and unavoidable today, because man now directs, plans, and programmes his history in quite a new way, and is called and bound to be responsible for it in futurology and world-wide planning, since he cannot otherwise continue to exist at all, yet knows that he is not justified in committing suicide collectively or individually. If in general history today by comparison with the past is in a radically new sense a *planned* history, then so too must be the history of the Church. And experiment in the narrower sense within the Church is the very way in which surrender to the incomprehensible, uncontrollable Lord of history *and* the duty of planning the future are united in a singular way: we attempt something new which is planned and we attempt it as provisional and relative and therefore revocable, since in this respect too we surrender ourselves to God's unknown future.

Creative experiment

What we have said – only in a very abstract way and without going into the arguments more precisely – about the nature of experiment properly so-called in the Church seems to be still far from being adequately recognized in the concrete life of the Church. For the most part, experiment is understood as dependent on a (more or less) express concession of the ecclesiastical legislator. And the latter offers only a certain choice of already (more or less) clearly known alternatives for experimentation, in order to decide which of them is better suited to a goal already fixed, so that the result cannot surprise the legislator. In his eyes the choice to be made as revealed by the experiment is purely selective, not creative; the result is the adaptation of something already existing and as such clearly known to a new situation (which we are determined from the beginning not to change, either because we simply cannot change it or because we are tired and think we can't): it is not the mutation of a being into a new entity (of course such analogies from natural history must be accepted only with reservations).

We frequently close ourselves up in the face of such experiments, if they become really serious, with an appeal to the unchangeable principles and convictions of Christianity. But even if we appeal to enduring basic convictions, the existence of which cannot be called in question (there are such and therefore they certainly have a permanent normative character for the Christian's actions and thus too for his experiments), nevertheless these principles are frequently understood in the light of a quite definite model of understanding (that of the *conversio ad phantasma* of scholastic philosophy: the intellect is said to turn to the concrete image acquired by sense-perception, 'abstract' from this what it has in common with other objects, and thus reach the 'universal' concept, so that there should be no conception without perception). This model is itself by no means a permanent element of the Christian principle and thus may exclude the experiment in question, although the principle as such would not exclude it.

We speak of respect for authority (which we may take to be an always valid principle) and mean in fact a quite definite form of this respect, which is not in fact eternally valid and thus does not without more ado forbid experiments in anti-authoritarian education. We speak of protecting the sacral element in the life of the Christian (which, rightly understood, certainly belongs to the notion of the Christian life) and mean a quite definite form of this sacral element, in a quite definite 'dosage', and as *starting* point of the understanding of the Christian life: a form which in reality is by no means an absolutely permanent factor in the Christian life and therefore can by no means forbid a somewhat desacralized Christian manner of life, or an experiment on these lines, so irrefutably as people often think.

The time-bound sense-perception can never be adequately separated in theoretical reflection from what is properly conceptually 'meant' by it: what we have are always merely ideas 'incarnated' in a particular temporal form and the distinction emerges, not from a purely theoretical 'abstraction', but from the transformation of the permanent essence from one temporal form to another – and this is just what happens in a real experiment. Only in real becoming do we come to know exactly the capacity for historical variation which the 'same' Christianity (if you like to call it that) possesses as its own, as belonging to this very 'sameness'. Christianity as way and hope of the absolute future must take this transforming mutation at least as seriously as what is 'permanent' in it.

It is only by experiment, taking a risk, feeling our way, that we learn whether a way of life, a thought-form, a terminology, and so on, are compatible or not with the 'permanent' element in Christianity, whether it would mean the death of Christianity (and therefore in the last resort would have to be rejected) or would be the very means – replacing the older means, tested by tradition – by which Christianity will stand its ground in a new age.

If Christianity then (as lived in the concrete) is pilgrimage, mutation, creation of the history of dogma (as introduction to all truth), through action and life, and if today this history is a history which is reflectively guided in a much higher sense than formerly (which is not to say that its goal is already adequately defined in advance), then experiment in the Church in the future is a permanent state, the representation and concrete expression of this Christian pilgrimage under the present-day conditions of reflection and planning, in the unavoidable quickening tempo of history.

Plea for responsible experiments

This is not an invitation to unplanned, wild experimenting, to arbitrariness in the Church, with everyone simply doing what he wants and calling it the inspiration of the Holy Spirit and a 'holy experiment'. But our reflections make clear the fact that the charismatic character of the Church means that not every experiment can be one organized or expressly permitted 'from above'. If there can be legitimate customs contrary to law, if justified paracanonical developments are possible, if there is something like a 'non-acceptance' of a law by the 'people' and not merely as a simple fact but as a legitimate procedure, then there can also be experiments which do not and in fact cannot have a preliminary official approval from above.

There are such experiments in theology. Any theologian who does not merely repeat the traditional formulas is experimenting on his own account and at his own risk: he is offering his theology to the Church, addressing to the Church the question whether her total awareness of faith can be recognized in this theology or not. This sort of thing is an experiment, since in fact, between this query and an answer, between offer and acceptance, there may be a long period of time during which the theology remains in the experimental stage.

There are many paracanonical developments in regional churches which are likewise meant as proposals to the whole Church, queries as to whether a particular practice could not be appropriately adopted by the Church as a whole. Such practices in ecclesiastical administration and pastoral care, if contrary to what is otherwise customary, have the character of an experiment at least in regard to the Church as a whole. The fact that the Church may possibly reject such an experiment after a certain time does not mean that it should never have been attempted. This sort of thing is involved in the very nature of experiment; otherwise it would not be an experiment. This too makes it clear once again that there is in principle nothing in the nature of a legitimate experiment which requires it to be expressly approved as such from the very beginning from above.

If then there can and should be experiments which do not first have to be approved, and yet not simply every sort of mad experiment is morally permissible, if we must distinguish , between experiments which are justified without preliminary approval and those which are merely arbitrary, and if this distinction cannot be made from the beginning by authority as such (as some nervous spirits in the Church think, for whom everything is forbidden which is not expressly permitted), then the distinction between the two kinds of experiment is a matter for a conscience which is self-critical while boldly sustaining its own responsibility and for charism in the Church: without these things the Church would degenerate into a bureaucratic apparatus and a totalitarian system. There is of course no denying the fact that recognition of the conscience which does not shelve its own responsibility and of the free charism can lead to some things 'happening' which would not happen under a totalitarian regime, that there is some unrest in the Church which gets on the nerves of sensitive and timid spirits. But in such unrest and out of it, in spite of all 'confusion', the Spirit of God, who is promised and given to the Church, has guaranteed to awaken the life that should be present, through *himself* and not through a cult of the norm and the letter of the law: a cult which would prevent any daring experiment from the start and thus render new life also impossible.

We must finally get used to the fact that in the Church too monolithism is not an ideal, that unrest, venture, and even an element of conflict belong in fact also to the life of the Church. If office-holders do not think that no one can raise a finger without their consent, that all experiments require approval in advance, and if those who perform unauthorized experiments do not think that they can never be rejected, but that every experiment is sacrosanct, then we can live also with unrest and struggle in a Church which must experiment and thus slowly find and practise for the future.

THE CHURCH'S
EUCHARISTIC CELEBRATION
AND THE CHRISTIAN'S
SUNDAY OBLIGATION

What can and must a dogmatic theologian say on this theme, if he has to be brief and yet act at the same time as representative also of the moral theologian?

1. The dogmatic theologian will certainly first of all be permitted to issue a warning against the possibility of over-estimating the sacramental element in the Church and therefore also the eucharistic celebration. We can of course, with Vatican II, call the Eucharist 'the summit toward which the activity of the Church is directed, at the same time the fountain from which all her power flows';[1] but we must also temper our commendation with theological caution and sobriety. For we can and must distinguish between the sign and what is signified – that is, between the cultic presence of the death of Christ and the death itself – and yet not simply separate the distinct factors. The Eucharist is fount and summit of the Christian life through what it signifies – the death of the Lord – and not merely within the dimension of the sacramental sign.

If we were to understand the statement of Vatican II – which gives expression to a liturgical enthusiasm widespread in recent decades – of the ritual happening as such, we would be glorifying a sacramentalism which it is precisely the task of Christianity to overcome, since salvation occurs everywhere in human existence through grace which is implanted into the whole of human existence in all its dimensions and reaches its real summit in the individual person at *that* point where faith, hope, and love are realized in the most decisive way : this is by no means necessarily and always precisely in worship.

This is not to deny that the eucharistic celebration has a privileged position in the life of the Christian and in the public life of the Church as such. But a warning must be issued against apotheoses of the Eucharist which are not theologically justified. We may be content simply to note that such apotheoses could in the long run only be detrimental from the standpoint of religious pedagogy for the understanding of Christianity.

2. In the light of the nature of the Church and of Christianity on the one hand and of the nature of the Eucharist on the other, the dogmatic and moral theologian will have to say with the whole of the Church's tradition that, in the normal case, the celebration of the Eucharist as the summit of the Church's self-realization in the dimension of her historicity and public, social life belongs irrevocably to the life of the Christian. The deliberate exclusion of all worship in principle and *a priori* would dissolve the Christian life as such and its ecclesial character. But this does not impose on the individual Christian any particular frequency for taking part in the Eucharist.

The obligation of attending Mass every Sunday arises from a positive commandment of the Church. The latter can of course be interpreted as the concrete realization of that fundamental reference of the Christian life to the eucharistic celebration which has already been mentioned. But as such it is and remains a commandment of the Church and nothing more. And, as long as it exists, it is open to that interpretation and to that peculiar form of observance which are appropriate to human ordinances, however important these may be. Such a commandment can be abolished in fact either by an explicit act of the legislator himself or by a contrary custom deemed to be legitimate in the moral consciousness of the people of God (at least of the greater part).

It is not for the dogmatic theologian to judge whether the stage has already been reached at which this human law could be abolished by a contrary universal custom. One obvious reason why I don't have to decide here is that in this respect circumstances differ in particular areas and among the various groups in the Church with their diverse mentalities. In any case it would be undesirable from the standpoint of religious pedagogy, in our part of the world, to continue to regard regular fulfilment of the Sunday obligation as *the* criterion of Church-membership and of Christian existence. How a Christian is 'practising' must be judged by more exact and more discriminating standards.

3. Contrary to an outlook widespread among Catholics but not always openly expressed, the dogmatic theologian must point out

that hearing God's word, its interpretation heard in faith, prayer, are not merely human events at most providing a kind of psychological preparation for the properly grace-bearing events of salvation: under the presuppositions also required for the reception of the sacraments, they are themselves real grace-bearing realizations of salvation which, even within the sacral sphere, cannot be restricted to the sacraments. This must be considered and taken seriously when the question is raised whether, from the standpoint of religion and religious education, in some or in many cases, it may not be desirable and better to offer, recommend, and recognize as fulfilling the 'Sunday obligation', instead of the Eucharist, some other happening in the sacral sphere ('sacral', however, in the comprehensive sense of the word just indicated). Since what is objectively the most significant in itself and what is here and now opportune and fruitful in human life very often do not coincide, since to what is sacrally significant and (under the necessary presuppositions) to the grace-bearing event of salvation everything belongs which occurs in faith, hope, and love, in the Church as such (therefore, not merely the Eucharist and the sacraments), there can be no dogmatic objections to a freely variable and alternative enlargement of the matter of the Sunday obligation.

4. In the light of the nature of the sacraments as suggested above and in view of the outlook prevailing in our secularized world of today, it would be very desirable and from the dogmatic standpoint also possible to interpret the sacraments and the Eucharist too not so much as events in which God's salvation-giving action enters in successive stages from outside into a world otherwise without grace and in this sense secular, but as events perceptible as signs and in the public life of the Church manifesting that endowment of grace and that dynamism oriented to the absolute future which God in his universal saving will has implanted in the whole world in all dimensions of human life. The Eucharist therefore would have to be understood as the symbolic observance (absolutely necessary and presenting in the sign the thing signified) of the death and resurrection of the Lord, in which God's grace pervading the whole world found its historical manifestation and was rendered eschatologically irreversible, which are effectively 'celebrated' in the whole life of the Christian, since everywhere

in it the suffering and death of the Lord are shared and the power of his resurrection experienced.

NOTE

1   Constitution on the Sacred Liturgy, ch. 1, para. 10. Abbot, p. 142.

SOURCES

THE GOSPEL CLAIM

'Righteousness in the New Testament'. Address to theology students at the College of St Charles Borromeo, Münster, 7.7.1968. Unpublished.

'Radical faith in ordinary life'. Sermon before the Catholic students' community in Münster, 5.7.1970. Unpublished.

'Man's possibilities and God's'. Sermon before the lay students of theology in Münster, 7.2.1969. Unpublished.

'Shrewd stewards of life'. Sermon in St Michael's, Munich, 28.7.1968. Unpublished.

MYSTERIES OF FAITH

'Advent as antidote to Utopia'. Unpublished.

'The cross – the world's salvation'. Meditations at the Catholic service on Good Friday, broadcast on Bavarian radio (1st programme), 27.3.1970. Unpublished.

'Risen victorious from the tomb'. Meditations for the Paschal Vigil, broadcast on Bavarian radio (1st programme), 28.3.1970.

'Easter'. Sermon in the Church of St Ignatius, Frankfurt-am-Main, during the Easter Mass on 6.4.1969, televised in Eurovision. Unpublished.

'Fear of the Spirit'. *Publik* No. 20, 15.5.1970

'Mary's Assumption'. Sermon on Bavarian radio, 15.8.1968. Unpublished.

FAITH AND PRAYER

'Theses on the theme: faith and prayer'. Prepared for a discussion at the Jesuit Curia in Rome. Published in *Geist und Leben* 42 (1969), pp. 177-84.

'On prayer today'. Script of a lecture to the Benedictine nuns of Holy Cross Abbey, Herstelle, 6.12.1968. Published in *Geist und Leben* 42 (1968), pp. 6-17; likewise *Christophorus* 14 (1969), No. 5; *Die Sendung* 22 (1969), No. 5, pp. 24-30.

'Prayer too is action'. Letter to Dutch Carmelite nuns, published in *Christliche Innerlichkeit* (Vienna), Jan.-Feb. 1969, pp. 1-2.

THE MESSAGE FOR TODAY

'What is the Christian message?' Working paper prepared for the international Concilium conference in Brussels (September, 1970). Unpublished.

'Theses on the problem of revelation and history'. Prepared for a lecture in the Ecumenical-theological working group (Evangelical-Catholic discussions) in Germany. Unpublished.

'Epochal mutation of Christian key-concepts'. Hitherto unpublished.

' "Sins" and guilt'. Unpublished.

'Peace as mandate'. Lecture at the annual meeting of the German women's circle on 12.11.1968, in Münster. Unpublished.

'Ordinary virtues'. *Geist und Leben* 43 (1970), pp. 46-47.

LIVING TESTIMONY

'Teresa of Avila: Doctor of the Church.' *Ecclesia* (Madrid) 30 (1970) of 26.9.1970, pp. 23-4 (in Spanish).

'Thinker and Christian. Obituary of Romano Guardini.' Broadcast on Bavarian radio (1st programme), 2.10.1968. Parts of this essay are taken from the obituary of Romano Guardini (cf. *Gnade als Freiheit*, Freiburg 1968, pp. 253f.).

'A man at play. Panegyric for Hugo Rahner'. Composed for an internal publication of the Jesuit order, published in *IHS* (Zürich) 1969, No. 2.

'Confidence and composure in sickness'. Sermon at the Mass broadcast by West-German radio from the church of the teaching hospital at the university of Münster on 21.6.1970. Unpublished.

'The doctor and Good Friday'. *Tribuna Medica* (Madrid) of 25.3.1970, pp. 14-15 (in Spanish).

PRIESTHOOD AND RELIGIOUS LIFE IN UPHEAVAL

'Current discussion on the celibacy of the secular priest: an answer'. Lecture at the conference of German-speaking rectors in Chur on 1.8.1948. First published in *Geist und Leben* 41 (1968), pp. 285-304.

'The meaning and justification of priestly celebrations'. *Mitten in der Gemeinde* (published by the Pontifical Work for Priestly Vocations), Munich 1968, pp. 13-19.

'The future of religious orders in the world and Church of today'. Lecture to Jesuits 23.9.1970 in Olpe. First published in *Geist und Leben* 43 (1970), pp. 338-54.

' "Making sacrifices" or everyday renunciation'. First published under the title 'Opfer und Öpferchen' in *Jetzt*, Munich, I (1970), pp. 3-5.

PILGRIM CHURCH

'Trust within the Church'. Sermon before lay students of theology in Münster on 25.6.1968. Unpublished.

'The duty of discussion. A plea for Cardinal Suenens.' *Publik*, 12.6.1970, pp. 23-4.

'Experiment in the field of Christianity and the Church'. *Internationale Dialogzeitschrift* 3 (1970), pp. 360-5.

'The Church's eucharistic celebration and the Christian's Sunday obligation'. One in a series of public lectures organized by the division of Catholic theology in the university of Münster 10.11.1970. Hitherto unpublished.